Pierre Loubier
Carlos Soldevila
Alexis de Gheldere

Travel better, enjoy more

Authors
Pierre Loubier
Contributors:
Carlos Soldevila
Alexis de Gheldere

Editor
Stéphane G.
Marceau

Publisher
Pascale Couture

Project Coordinator
Jacqueline Grekin

Copy Editing
Jacqueline Grekin
Anne Joyce
Editing Assistance
Dena Duijkers

Translation
Suzanne Murray
Francesca Worrall
Janet Logan

Page Layout
Typesetting
Dena Duijkers
Visuals
Isabelle Lalonde

Cartographers
André Duchesne
Bradley Fenton
Patrick Thivierge
Yanik Landreville

Computer Graphics
Stéphanie Routhier

Artistic Director
Patrick Farei (Atoll)

Illustrations
Dominique Morin-
Loubier
Lorette Pierson
Myriam Gagné

Photography
Cover Page
Tibor Bognár
Inside Pages
Patrick Escudero
Pierre Loubier

OFFICES
CANADA: Ulysses Travel Guides, 4176 Rue St-Denis, Montréal, Québec, H2W 2M5,
☎ (514) 843-9447 or 1-877-542-7247, ⇌(514) 843-9448, info@ulysses.ca,
www.ulyssesguides.com

EUROPE: Les Guides de Voyage Ulysse SARL, BP 159, 75523 Paris Cedex 11, France,
☎ 01 43 38 89 50, ⇌01 43 38 89 52, voyage@ulysse.ca, www.ulyssesguides.com

U.S.A.: Ulysses Travel Guides, 305 Madison Avenue, Suite 1166, New York, NY 10165,
☎ 1-877-542-7247, info@ulysses.ca, www.ulyssesguides.com

DISTRIBUTORS
CANADA: Ulysses Books & Maps, 4176 Saint-Denis, Montréal, Québec, H2W 2M5,
☎ (514) 843-9882, ext.2232, 800-748-9171, Fax: 514-843-9448, info@ulysses.ca,
www.ulyssesguides.com

GREAT BRITAIN AND IRELAND: World Leisure Marketing, Unit 11, Newmarket Court,
Newmartket Drive, Derby DE24 8NW, ☎ 1 332 57 37 37, Fax: 1 332 57 33 99
office@wlmsales.co.uk

SCANDINAVIA: Scanvik, Esplanaden 8B, 1263 Copenhagen K, DK, ☎ (45) 33.12.77.66,
Fax: (45) 33.91.28.82

SPAIN: Altaïr, Balmes 69, E-08007 Barcelona, ☎ 454 29 66, Fax: 451 25 59,
altair@globalcom.es

SWITZERLAND: Havas Services Suisse, ☎(26) 460 80 60, fax: (26) 460 80 68

U.S.A.: The Globe Pequot Press, 246 Goose Lane, Guilford, CT 06437 - 0480,
☎1-800-243-0495, Fax: 800-820-2329, sales@globe-pequot.com

Other countries, contact Ulysses Books & Maps, 4176 Rue Saint-Denis, Montréal, Québec,
H2W 2M5, ☎ (514) 843-9882, ext.2232, 800-748-9171, Fax: 514-843-9448, info@ulysses.ca,
www.ulyssesguides.com

Canadian Cataloguing-in-Publication Data (see page 4)
© September 2000, Ulysses Travel Guides.
All rights reserved Printed in Canada
ISBN 2-89464-320-9

"At a time when the mother country believed that the art of governing colonies consisted of setting up batteries of cannons, it planned the construction of Havana's city walls, begun at the beginning of the 17th century and completed in the late 18th century. The walls, part of the vast overall fortifications, surrounded the city both towards the mainland and the sea and port. The fortification was endowed with four gates leading to the countryside, posterns towards the sea, drawbridges, deep ditches, esplanades, arsenals, palisades, loopholes and castellated bastions. As a result, the most populated city on the island was transformed into an immense fortress."

Cirilo Villaverde, *Cecilia Valdés*,
published in Havana in 1839
(Our translation)

Write to Us

The information contained in this guide was correct at press time. However, mistakes can slip in, omissions are always possible, places can disappear, etc. The authors and publisher hereby disclaim any liability for loss or damage resulting from omissions or errors.

We value your comments, corrections and suggestions, as they allow us to keep each guide up to date. The best contributions will be rewarded with a free book from Ulysses Travel Guides. All you have to do is write us at the following address and indicate which title you would be interested in receiving (see the list at the end of guide).

Ulysses Travel Guides
4176 Rue Saint-Denis
Montréal, Québec
Canada H2W 2M5
www.ulysses.ca
E-mail: text@ulysses.ca

Cataloguing

Canadian Cataloguing-in-Publication Data

Loubier, Pierre
   Havana
   (Ulysses travel guide)
   Translation of: La Havane
   Includes index.
   ISBN 2-89464-320-9
   1. Havana (Cuba) - Guidebooks. I. Title. II. Collection.
F1799.H33L6813 2000   917.291'240464   C00-941560-2

Thanks

We acknowledge the financial support of the Government of Canada through the Book Publishing Industry Development Program (BPIDP) for our publishing activities.

We would also like to thank SODEC (Québec) for its financial support.

Thanks to: M. Jorge Alvarez (Cuban Tourism Bureau), Ms. Yaquelyn Triana Gomez (Publicitur, Havana) and M. Carlos Javier Santamarina (Habaguanex, Havana).

Table of Contents

List of Maps

Map Symbols

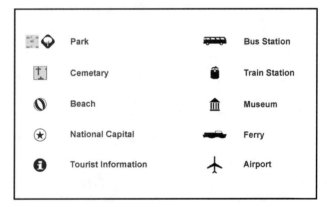

Park			Bus Station
Cemetary			Train Station
Beach			Museum
National Capital			Ferry
Tourist Information			Airport

Symbols

🛶	Ulysses's Favourite
☎	Telephone Number
⇄	Fax Number
≡	Air Conditioning
⊗	Fan
≈	Pool
ℜ	Restaurant
ℝ	Refrigerator
K	Kitchenette
tv	Television
ctv	Cable Television
pb	Private Bathroom
sb	Shared Bathroom
bkfst incl.	Breakfast Included
FAP	Full American Plan

ATTRACTION CLASSIFICATION

★	Interesting
★★	Worth a visit
★★★	Not to be missed

HOTEL CLASSIFICATION

The prices in the guide are for one room, double occupancy in high season.

RESTAURANT CLASSIFICATION

$	$12 or less
$$	$12 to $21
$$$	$22 and more

The prices in the guide are for a meal for one person, not including drinks and tip.

All prices in this guide are in US dollars.

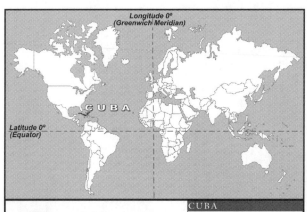

Where is Havana?

CUBA
Capital: Havana
Language: Spanish
Population: 11,000,000 inhab.
Currency: Cuban peso
Area: 110,922 km² (42, 816 sq)

HAVANA
Population : 2,200,000
Area: 727 km² (281 sq mi)

Longitude 0°
(Greenwich Meridian)

Latitude 0°
(Equator)

CUBA

Mexico

CUBA

Dominican
Republic

Haiti

Puerto Rico

Jamaica

Belize

Honduras

Guatemala

El Salvador

Nicaragua

Caribbean Sea

Costa Rica

Panama

Venezuela

Pacific
Ocean

Colombia

Ecuador

Peru

Brazil

©ULYSSES

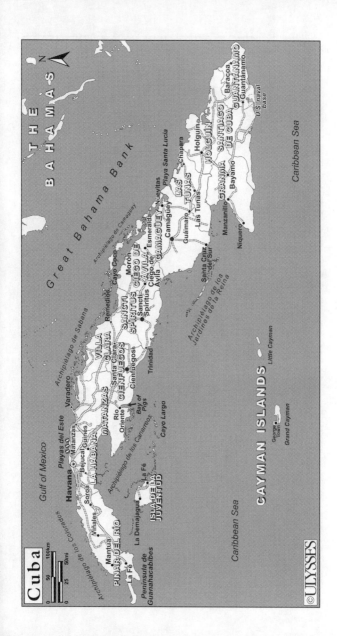

Cuba

0 50 100km
0 25 50mi

© ULYSSES

Gulf of Mexico

Archipiélago de los Colorados

Mantua
La Fé
PINAR DEL RÍO
Viñales
Soroa
Playas del Este
Havana
Bejucal
Güines
LA HABANA
Varadero
Matanzas
MATANZAS
Río
Oriente
Bay of Pigs
Cienfuegos
CIENFUEGOS
Trinidad
Archipiélago de Sabana
Santa Clara
VILLA CLARA
Remedios
SANCTI SPÍRITUS
Sancti Spíritus
Morón
Cayo Coco
CIEGO DE ÁVILA
Ciego de Ávila

La Demajagua
La Fé
ISLA DE LA JUVENTUD

Peninsula de Guanahacabibes

Archipiélago de los Canarreos
Cayo Largo

CAYMAN ISLANDS

Caribbean Sea

George Town
Grand Cayman
Little Cayman

Great Bahama Bank

THE BAHAMAS

Archipiélago de Camagüey
Esmeralda
Nuevitas
Camagüey
CAMAGÜEY
Guáimaro
Santa Cruz del Sur
Playa Santa Lucía
Chaparra
LAS TUNAS
Las Tunas
Manzanillo
GRANMA
Bayamo
Níquero
HOLGUÍN
Holguín
SANTIAGO DE CUBA
Baracoa
GUANTÁNAMO
Guantánamo
U.S. naval base

Archipiélago de los Jardines de la Reina

Caribbean Sea

N

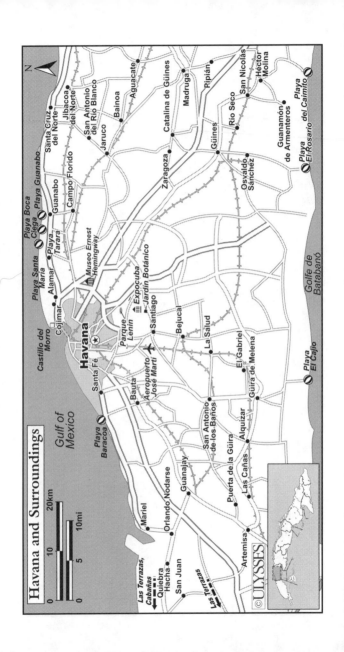

Havana and Surroundings

N

Gulf of Mexico

Golfe de Batabanó

0   10   20km
0   5   10mi

© ULYSSES

Las Terrazas, Cabañas
Quiebra Hacha
San Juan
Las Terrazas

Mariel
Orlando Nodarse
Guanajay
Artemisa

Playa Baracoa
Santa Fé
Bauta
Aeropuerto José Martí
Puerta de la Güira
Las Cañas
San Antonio de los Baños
Alquízar
Güira de Melena

Castillo del Morro
Cojímar
Playa Santa María
Alamar
Playa Tarará
Museo Ernest Hemingway

Havana
Parque Lenin
Santiago
Jardín Botánico
Expocuba
Bejucal
El Gabriel
La Salud

Playa Boca Ciega
Playa Guanabo
Guanabo
Campo Florido

Santa Cruz del Norte
Jibacoa del Norte
San Antonio del Río Blanco
Jaruco
Aguacate
Bainoa

Catalina de Güines
Madruga
Zaragoza
Güines
Pipián
San Nicolás

Río Seco
Osvaldo Sánchez
Guanamón de Armentero

Héctor Molina
Playa El Rosario
Playa del Caimito

Playa El Cajío

Portrait

The first thing that strikes visitors on arriving in Havana is its urbanity.

Not a false, superficial urbanity, but one that is deeply rooted in its very walls, its way of life and its population of over two-million inhabitants. Lest we forget, Havana was once the third great city of the Americas, surpassed only by Lima and Mexico City, and still retains traces of its past grandeur.

The strategic position of Havana, the "gateway to the New World," and its rich and fertile interior have made it a melting pot of cultures, giving the city unsurpassable charm. The old city recalls the Spanish occupation that steered the island's destiny for close to 400 years. The Vedado emphasizes the U.S. presence, whose influence was more profound than it appears. And the rhythm of the West Indies pulses in its multiracial population whose Af

rican soul is well at home here. The character and fascination of Havana come from the mix of these three cultural trends that have achieved a truly unique balance here.

And as if this were not enough, there is the

Revolution, which led the city to the threshold of modern history and still wraps it in an aura of mystery, infusing us with the desire to know more, to understand more.

All this makes Havana a particularly rich destination. The city is more than the sum of its monuments, palaces, fortresses and promenades. It is an ambiance, an atmosphere in which indifference has not yet taken hold.

Geography

Havana is located in western Cuba, the largest of the Antilles. Almost level with the Tropic of Cancer, on one of the northernmost points of the island, it stands like a sentinel at the entrance to the Gulf of Mexico. It lies a mere 180km (112mi) south of the U.S. state of Florida and less than 500km (311mi) from the shores of the Yucatan peninsula, in Mexico.

Considered one of the 14 provinces of the Cuban archipelago, Havana covers a surface area of 727km² (281 sq. mi). It is built around a large bay that determined its development on an east-west axis into districts marked by its turbulent history.

Habana Vieja (Old Havana), Centro Habana, the Vedado and Miramar, on the sea front, harbour most of the capital's cultural and tourist attractions. Finding your way around is easy thanks to its wide thoroughfares and network of streets laid out in a U.S.-style grid pattern.

History

Though caves containing traces of pre-Columbian (most likely Ciboney Indian) occupation have been discovered near Havana, the history of the city itself only really begins with the arrival of the Spanish in this part of the archipelago.

Discovery

One of seven near-mythical cities founded by Diego Velázquez in 1514 – 22 years after Christopher Columbus "discovered" the island – San Cristobal de La Habana was first established on the island's south coast, in the vicinity of the present-day port of Batabano. The insalubrity of the site, as well as the new direction of empire affairs after the "discovery" of Mexico, convinced the powers that be of the need to relocate the colony to the other side of the isthmus. The large bay "discovered" by Sebastian de Ocampo in 1508 when he first circumnavigated the island was then chosen.

Galleon

Briefly set up near the Rio Almedares, between the contemporary Vedado and Miramar, the settlement soon moved a little farther east and was established for good at its present harbour-mouth location. After a few years of fluctuating prosperity, this location would become the most important and best-protected port of the Spanish empire. The first Catholic mass in Havana was held on December 17, 1519, in the heart of the original city, near the present-day Plaza de Armas.

Pre-eminence

Havana's first vocation was a function of its geographical position. Its location at the entrance to the Gulf of Mexico and its remarkable natural harbour quickly attracted the attention of the Spanish authorities. From a simple logistical base for the conquest of the continent, a conquest to which the city devoted its first efforts, it took on a resolutely military character the moment the riches of the New World began to flow toward Europe.

Since this natural harbour was the last major port before the long voyage across the Atlantic, it soon became a regular stopping point and supply base for Spanish ships heading into the Gulf Stream on their way back to Spain. The haphazard traffic of the ships, however, made them particularly vulnerable. Repeated attacks by pirates lured by the treasure-laden galleons soon made necessary a certain coordination of total strength. The convoy system was thus spawned, defining the city's rhythm for many years to come.

Institutionalized in 1564, the convoys were organized around two great Atlantic fleets, the famous *flotas* of Mexico and Peru. Escorted

Portrait

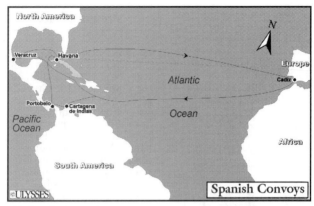

Spanish Convoys

©ULYSSES

by mighty warships, the cargo-ship convoy gathered every spring in the port of Havana before sailing across the ocean with its spoils. The city thus became a beehive of activity for more than six weeks out of the year. The maintenance of ships, supplying of foodstuffs and a whole array of related services grew rapidly to meet the needs of vessels and their crews.

The city blossomed thanks to this fleet-service-based industry. A mixed population with convergent interests settled around the large bay. The first buildings to mark Havana's landscape were made of wood, doing nothing to deter the pirates who readily came to attack ships berthed in the harbour. The city was even torched twice – in 1538 and 1555 – a victim of its fame.

But all this changed as soon as the Spanish crown realized the strategic importance of Havana and its harbour. From that moment on, the mother country worked to provide the city with fortifications that measured up to the role it had just been assigned: "fortress of the Indies," guardian of the Gulf of Mexico and the main maritime routes between the Old World and the New.

Portrait

Convoys

The routes taken by Spanish ships between the New and Old Worlds were well mapped out by the middle of the 16th century. They were strictly defined, taking into account the currents and prevailing winds (see map). But it is this high degree of predictability that made the vessels of the Spanish fleet so vulnerable, and the idea of regrouping the ships and have them escorted by armed galleons thus naturally evolved out of this observation.

Organization into convoys seems to have been remarkably efficient. Only twice did this system prove incapable of defending the Empire's treasures: once in 1628, when a Dutch fleet of 31 vessels seized the Mexican fleet of 20 ships off Matanzas, a little east of Havana; and another time in 1656, when English pirates captured several ships of the Peruvian fleet approaching the Spanish port of Cadiz before seizing that of New Spain, which had taken refuge in the Azores.

The first stone structures had a resolutely defensive character. The Castillo de La Fuerza, completed in 1577, and, on either side of the narrow entrance to the bay, the La Punta and El Morro fortresses, both started 20 years later, were designed to protect the city and its harbour. Until 1674, when a rampart around the city was completed, Havana's martial appearance became increasingly obvious.

The importance granted Havana by the mother country soon ensured its pre-eminence over the entire Cuban archipelago. In

1556, it replaced Santiago de Cuba as the headquarters of the general harbour master's office, and was promoted to the rank of the colony's capital in 1607. Moreover, this concentration of power was greatly reinforced by the mother country's mercantile policy, which gave the city the exclusive right to conduct business with Spain.

So it was that at the turn of the 18th century, close to half of Cuba's 20,000 inhabitants lived in Havana. A provincial city that was more impressive for its military reputation than its elegance (or lack thereof), it nonetheless managed to make a name for itself as the political and economic centre of the island. A mere dependency of the viceroyalty of Mexico, its existence was then intimately linked to that of the empire from which it drew support and protection. But the city was never to deny its origins, even if it meant being pitted against the rest of the colony.

Divergences

The provisions needed for armadas gave local agriculture its initial commercial outlet. First centred on essential foodstuffs, it soon developed into more specialized production to meet the demand of markets beyond the island itself. Tobacco, coffee and sugar began to stand out as sources of revenue independent of the empire's specific demands. A new, mostly Creole, farming class grew quickly on this basis; a class of people with its own distinct interests.

The land stretching from Havana to the back country was systematically cultivated and the income derived from it gave the colony a certain boost. Despite this, the mother country decided to tighten its previously loosely applied trade policies. And, as of 1700, Bourbon Spain chose a direction that would soon rouse the ire of planters.

In 1717, the Spanish crown established a monopolistic corporation known as "Factoria de Tabacos" to regulate the tobacco trade, which was then the colony's main cash crop. Consequently, Cuban tobacco had to be sold to authorized representatives at fixed prices. A quota system was established to guarantee the value of the goods on the European market by limiting production, which had disastrous consequences for the nascent industry.

As Havana was the administrative centre of the island,

it was through this city that Seville (the centre of Spanish colonial trade at the time) applied its orders. Havana's submission to the empire's demands was becoming flagrant, much like the benefits it derived from the situation. The *peninsulares*, Spaniards employed by the mother country or merchants with business permits, grew richer through this system, which funnelled the colony's resources into their hands. They became the city's dominant class and fiercely defended their privileges.

In August 1717, this prompted over 500 *vegueros* (tobacco producers) to march against Havana, the city that had opposed their interests. Well armed, the Creole *vegueros* forced the Factoria de Tabacos to suspend operations as well as the resignation of the colony's governor general. However, the Creole planters' victory over the mother country was short-lived.

After reinforcing the garrison, Spain reinstated the Factoria de Tabacos, which resumed its activities in 1720. In the years that followed, the *vegueros* twice took up arms against the implementation of monopolistic trade policies. The second time, they were expected. The governor

general turned the militia on the hapless planters, a number of whom died in battle or were executed in the following weeks.

Victorious, Spain soon extended its imperial trading monopoly over all the island's goods by setting up the Real Compania de Comercio in 1740. The tone was set. Commercial Havana would consequently oppose the producing colony. An unforseen event settled differences for some time, but the rivalry between the city's interests and those of the interior would henceforth shape the colony's history.

Liberalization

In 1756, the hegemonic war that opposed European powers extended beyond its natural framework. The Seven Years' War (1756-1763) ensnared the Americas in a conflict laden with consequences. When Spain joined France in its fight against England, an English attack on Havana was the unfortunate outcome, changing the city forever.

After two relentless months, the British finally obtained the city's surrender on August 14, 1762, and took refuge in Havana for nearly a year until the British government accepted the hand-over of the island to Spain in exchange for Florida. As a result of these months of occupation, the colony's trade system was completely overhauled.

Great defenders of free trade, the British removed all restrictions on the circulation of goods. A period of intense economic activity ensued, and Havana's merchants were the first to benefit. From England and the 13 North American colonies came goods that until then could not be found or were too expensive. The demand for such things as cereal, tools, farm machinery and slaves was insatiable. In 10 months, over 1,000 ships anchored in the Havana harbour.

But it wasn't just the demand for products that increased. The British occupation also opened an immense market for the colony's export products. Coffee, sugar, tobacco and leather could suddenly be traded freely under conditions that were more advantageous than ever.

Production augmented prodigiously thanks in part to the importation of a submissive workforce on which it increasingly depended. When Spain took control of the island once again, it was evident that there was no turning back. In fact, the Empire itself was in full mutation. King Charles III, a liberal at heart, ordered the abolition of monopolies and a review of the taxation of colonial products. In 1756, Havana was granted the right to trade with six cities on the Iberian peninsula and later, with most ports in the Spanish Indies.

Obviously, this deregulation ended the need for the convoy system which had once determined the city's role in the Empire but was now little more than a hindering relic of the past. Havana was making its entrance into the realm of international trade.

The increase in trade that followed the British takeover helped Havana establish its predominance over the fertile lands of the island's interior by emphasizing the region's function as intermediary. Since Cuba was on the verge of a period of opulence, the city was certainly well placed to reap the benefits.

Golden Age

Two major events at the end of the 18th century had extremely important consequences for Havana. The rebellion of the British colonies (destined to become the United States of America in 1776) provided Cuba with a market in full expansion. By taking over the trade of tropical products with the dissenters from the British colonies in the Indies, commerce in Cuba reached such gargantuan proportions that the port had to be rebuilt so that it could accommodate some 200 ships which sailed from North America every year.

However, it was primarily the 1791 slave uprising in San Domingo that propelled Cuba to prosperity. The resulting destruction of the colony's sugar infrastructure cut Europe off abruptly from its main sugar supply, causing both the demand for and the price of sugar to skyrocket. Separated from San Domingo on its eastern seaboard by a 65km (40mi) channel, the Spanish colony of Cuba welcomed nearly 30,000 French settlers who arrived with their slaves, capital and expertise. Under these conditions, Cuba was ready to become the new chief sugar producer.

More black slaves were imported and the modest sugar industry, which began in the middle of the 17th century, especially around the capital, increased its production at staggering rates. The 100 presses on the island in the early 1700s were multiplied by five in 1792, by 10 in 1827 and finally, by 20 in 1868. During this last year, the island supplied close to 30% of the sugar on the world market. The sugar tyranny took root on the island.

For Havana, this was a godsend. As the island's main port city, it was the only one with the proper infrastructure to handle the abundant sugar harvests. The industry thus flourished by the sea close to the city. Until the first railways were built in the late 1830s, the sea was virtually the only way to transport goods to the capital of the Cuban archipelago.

The exceptional level of development that marked this period caused the heart of the city to expand. Walls surrounding Havana were torn down so that it could spread out comfortably. With nearly 40% of the colony's population (approximately 125,000 people), Havana had more inhabitants at the turn of the 19th century than Boston, New York or Philadelphia.

Portrait

The Prado's bronze lion

Bordered on the east by its large harbour, the city unfurled westward with the construction of its most beautiful architectural creations. The Paseo del Prado, a promenade to rival any in the metropolises of Europe, was just the beginning for a city that better suited the aspirations of an affluent elite. The private hotels of this new bourgeoisie, mostly important landowners and rich merchants, gathered ostentatiously around Parque Central, the hub of the new Havana. Public lighting, urban transportation, telephones and electricity were provided, just like in the great modern cities of the world. But Havana's grand new airs could not hide old animosities.

Independence Wars

The prosperity brought on by sugar had its share of downfalls as well, and the city's economic growth fueled the increasing tension between the metropolis and the colony. A large segment of the population began to feel smothered by the imperial structure. Because of the metropolis's discriminating policies, the Creoles were restricted to farming and increasingly subjected by monoculture for export markets over which they had no control.

From the mercantilism of yesteryear, Spain still maintained the power to control tariffs, allowing it to promote its own interests and to direct some of the profits into its own coffers. The situation worsened considerably during the second half of the 19th century when commercial ties between Cuba and Spain dwindled, while those linking Cuba to the United States were stronger than ever. Between 1850 and 1877, trade with the United States increased from 39% to 82% of the colony's economic activity whereas, during the same period, trade with Spain slipped from 27% to 6%. In light of these circumstances, it became difficult to justify the imperial policies that restrained the colony's development and benefited only the motherland and its offspring, the *peninsulares*.

For the most part, the Creole people simply demanded representation in the Spanish government and reforms to the tax and tariff system. Worried that the dissolution of the colonial association would sound the death knell for slavery, the base of their wealth, the Creole population was generally more reformist than revolutionary. For several years, they voiced their grievances in a peaceful manner, only to encounter contempt and misunderstanding. In the end, the Spanish completely shut them out of the governor's palace, provoking the birth of a radical movement

that soon escalated into armed conflict.

First Attempt

The Ten Years' War broke out in 1768 when Creole planter Carlos Manuel de Céspedes freed his slaves and, from his land in the Oriente, near Bayamo, proclaimed the colony's independence. Spain responded promptly to this provocation by sending 100,000 armed men to the island. This was the biggest colonial conflict since the wars liberating the colonies from the continent. Within 10 years, this war would result in nearly 250,000 deaths and throw the country's economy into a slump from which it would have great difficulty recovering.

From the onset of this conflict, the island was divided in two. Wealthier, more dependent on slavery and with strong ties to Havana, planters in the west worried that the policies of the temporary Céspedes government would upset their lifestyle. They refused to join the rebels, thus putting an end to this first revolt against the metropolis.

Spain hastened to make use of this divergence between the planters. Quickly reacting to limit the threat to its domination, Spain literally cut Cuba in half. Between

The Martyrs of 1871

Without a doubt, the episode that had the greatest impact on Havana during this period was the execution of eight medical students accused of defacing the tombstone of Gonzalo Castanon, founder of the pro-Spanish newspaper *La Voz de Cuba*. This harsh sentence would haunt Cubans for a long time. A monument commemorating the students was erected east of the Prado, in the Parque Martires del 71. It was built with the remnants of the wall against which the victims were lined up and shot.

Moron and Jucaro, in Ciego de Avila, it erected a forti-fied line called the *trocha* that crossed the isthmus from one end to the other, separating the "good" seed from the "bad."

As a result, the sugar-cane industry in the eastern part of the archipelago was al-most completely destroyed; the west, however, was saved. As for Havana, it was relatively unaffected by the conflict. Centre of Spanish power, controlled by the *peninsulares* and thousands of soldiers in transit, the city did not let conflict trouble its best years. It continued to adorn itself with magnifi-cent buildings that can still be admired today, and re-mained undaunted by the few brutal explosions that disturbed the rest of the island.

Second Attempt

With the Oriente ravaged, Spain ended the conflict in 1878 by promising to re-view the colony's political and economic system. The Zanjòn Agreement instituted a very precarious peace, which was soon shaken by the island's economic diffi-culties.

The war had cost the col-ony an important share of the market at the worst time possible. While battles raged on in Cuba, new sugar suppliers emerged. Latin America was becom-ing a large-scale producer, and Europe too joined in on the adventure thanks to the sugar-beet culture. Prices diminished, and the Cuban economy collapsed. The ensuing depression provided the backdrop for the second uprising against Havana.

The second war of independence was instigated in early 1895 by Cuban intellectual José Marti. As an eminent figure respected across Spanish America, this *Habanero*, who spent most of his adult life in exile, provided cohesion and an ideological framework for the insurrection. Marti, soon nicknamed "the apostle of freedom", was killed in one of the very first confrontations. But his strong influence attracted the majority of Cubans to the ideals of revolt. He endowed Cuban nationalism with a body of ideas that ensured its perenniality.

This time, the whole island was inflamed. The revolt no longer solely concerned the planters. The bourgeoisie, the urban-working class, the peasantry – in short, all the people of Cuba – were stirred by the agitation. The war struck the very foundations of Cuban society.

It soon become clear that nothing could stop the movement and that Spain was losing the battle. The *peninsulares* took refuge on the outskirts of the city, in a desperate attempt to survive the upheaval, but panic overcame reason. As the metropolis prepared to extricate itself from the conflict in late 1897, Havana was the stage for a final loyalist outbreak.

Riots broke out in the city when General "Butcher" Weyler was dismissed from duty. Many saw Weyler as the ultimate defender of the imperial order and integrity. Weyler was responsible for the all-out war policy as well as the "reconcentration" camps, *reconcentrados*, where thousands of Cuban civilians perished. As soon as his discharge became public, the city streets filled with military personnel and citizens enraged by what they considered a conciliatory gesture on the part of the Spanish authorities. The uprising reached such heights of violence that the United States, concerned for the safety of its citizens and its interests, dispatched the *U.S.S. Maine* battleship to Havana's harbour. Nobody could have predicted the consequences that such an action would have on the Spanish presence in Cuba, anymore than on the profound aspirations of Cuban patriots.

Enter the United States

The United States had already been on the verge of intervention for some time. Washington was very interested in what was happening in Cuba. Indeed, events in Cuba had always been of utmost interest to Washington. Once again, the geographic location of the island was to seal its fate.

Soon after the American War of Independence, President Jefferson stated that the only way to ensure the protection of Cuba was by annexing it. In the 1820s, in the wake of the "Louisiana Purchase" (1803) and the purchase of Florida (1819), then Secretary of State John Quincy Adams exposed his political gravitation theory, which would leave its mark on U.S.-Cuban policy for the rest of the century. His theory stipulated that just as the law of gravity governed the physical world, a similar law governed the political world. As the apple torn from its tree by a storm could only fall to the ground, Cuba, once detached from Spain, could only slide under the thumb of the United States, which needed only to be patient and wait for the fruit to ripen before plucking it.

The obvious destiny now revealed its full extent.

However, Adams's successors did not have his patience. On two occasions, in 1848 and in 1854, the United States tried to buy Cuba from Spain, first for $100 million, then for $130 million, to no avail. The United States also counted on the annexationist sentiment that was growing among members of the Cuban elite, going so far as to tolerate some of their romantic whims of conquest, such as the three attempts by Narciso Lopez, father of the Cuban flag.

Midway through the 19th century, however, it was by introducing capital that the United States invested the island. Soon after the first war of independence, the United States hastened to buy at low prices the great plantations of the Oriente that had been abandoned by owners who were unable to continue cultivating. These properties were to form the heart of the economic takeover of Cuba.

By sending the *U.S.S. Maine* to Havana, the United States demonstrated that its interest was real and persistent. The people of the United States, fed by the media for months, supported and encouraged their

"Remember the Maine"

Although it wasn't one of the most important ships in the U.S. Navy, the *U.S.S. Maine* was nevertheless one of the first steel battleships powered by steam engines. Well-armed, this floating fortress had 354 crew members and officers aboard.

The U.S. president ordered this ship to Havana on January 24, 1898, after riots shook the Cuban capital. For months, the U.S. Consul had been urgently asking the government to send a warship to the city's port to protect U.S. interests in the country.

Stationed in the southern Florida Keys, the *U.S.S. Maine* had been awaiting this order for some time. Once it was received, the *Maine* took only five hours to cross the Florida Strait. At 9am on January 25, the ship arrived in the Havana harbour on a courtesy visit.

The Spanish authorities played along admirably and avoided any kind of confrontation. The officers of the *Maine* were treated with respect, and sailors were allowed to come and go freely. However, under the veneer of such civility, a blatant mistrust brewed and the arrival of the *Maine* in the capital was perceived as a provocation.

Three uneventful weeks passed. And then, on February 15 at 9:40pm two explosions shook the port. The *U.S.S. Maine* burned for over four hours before sinking 40ft (12m), bringing with it 260 crew members and three officers. It was the worst disaster in the history of the U.S. Navy.

At first, no one was blamed for the tragedy. But before any investigation could take place, headlines in the U.S. press accused Spain. William Randolph Hearst's *New York Journal* became the voice of the entire nation and demanded that the U.S. avenge this affront by immediately declaring war. To the cries of "Remember the Maine," the United States eagerly disposed of what remained of Spain's colonial domain on the brink of collapse.

In Havana in 1925, the United States dedicated a monument to the victims of the *Maine* in an ultimate bid to justify their presence on Cuban soil. However, soon after the Revolution, this symbol of the Yankee presence was seriously damaged by the people. The bronze eagle that adorned it can now be observed at the Museo de la Revolucion in Havana.

government's interventionist policy.

As a result, when a terrible explosion destroyed the *U.S.S. Maine* in the Havana harbour on February 15, 1898, no one missed the call. "Remember the Maine" became the war cry of a nation that had been waiting for weeks to display its anger. Thus began the "splendid little war" that put Cuba under the yoke of the United States for over half a century.

Seizure

It took only 113 days for the United States to claim victory. On July 3, the Spanish Atlantic fleet was destroyed in the bay of Santiago de Cuba, ending a conflict whose outcome had been clear from the start.

In accordance with the Treaty of Paris, signed on December 10, 1898, the Philippines, Puerto Rico and Guam were annexed to the North American Republic. Cuba's case was particular, however. Spain had ceded the island to the United States, but the latter had managed to get itself in a difficult situation. While the U.S. Congress discussed the act allowing armed forces to be sent to Cuba, a weighty amendment was proposed by Senator Teller of Colorado. Ultimately included in the final text, this amendment stipulated

Portrait

that the United States of America recognized Cuba's right to independence and specified that U.S. troops withdraw from the country as soon as a constitutionally elected government took over.

Although the U.S. position was delicate, it was never a question of simply handing back to the Cubans the island that they had fought over for 30 years. When Spain's official surrender ceremony took place in the summer of 1898, it was not a Cuban flag that flew over Havana, but a U.S. one. Cuban soldiers were not even allowed to enter the capital to see the Spanish walk, for the last time after 400 years of domination, towards the harbour.

January 1, 1899 was the beginning of a military occupation that would last three years. The argument invoked to justify this brutal act: the Cubans' inability to govern themselves. There was no serious opposition to this takeover. The colony was out of breath. War had devastated the entire island and now that the Spanish were gone, it was harder than ever to pinpoint the enemy. This wouldn't last long.

Washington's policy regarding Cuba took the shape of a symbol of neo-colonialism

known as the Platt Amendment. Imposed on the national congress elected in 1900 with 5% of the population allowed to vote based on norms set by Washington, then included in the 1901 Cuban constitution under the threat of a prolonged occupation, the Platt Amendment had eight clauses. The amendment's main stipulations included: the limited right to sign treaties with independent states or to obtain international loans; Cuba's obligation to sell or rent a part of its territory for the creation of a U.S. naval base; and the right of the United States to militarily intervene to defend its interests or to protect the life, property or individual freedom of the island's inhabitants.

The meaning of all this was quite clear. General Leonard Wood, who headed the occupation government, summarized the situation in a letter to Vice-President Roosevelt:

"There is, of course, little or no real independence left to Cuba under the Platt Amendment...; she is absolutely in our hands and I believe that no European government for a moment considers that she is otherwise than a practical dependency of the United States...."

The significance of this amendment did not elude

the Cuban people. Havana revolted the day after its content was divulged. Public meetings, processions in the streets and mass assemblies indicated that no one was indifferent to what had just taken place. The United States had stolen Cuba's right to autonomy. For nearly 40 years, the Platt Amendment would unite the islanders in a virulent opposition and lend a bitter taste to U.S.-Cuban relations.

The Republic

In May 1902, the occupation government finally surrendered the island's administration to the Cuban people. Tomas Estrada Palma, a Quaker who spent 20 years teaching in the United States, became the first president of the Republic of Cuba. But Palma inherited a republic ruined by war, and limited powers.

The Cuban government's first actions certainly did not encourage the autonomists. In 1903, Guantanamo was handed over to the United States and became a naval base. In the same vein, the Platt Amendment was added to a "permanent treaty" that closely linked the two countries. Heaping insult on injury, a commercial reciprocity treaty gave the United States economic

control over all island trade through the application of a series of preferential tariffs.

These initiatives led to a vast movement of U.S. capital that swept over the island. The right of intervention sanctioned by the Platt Amendment became a kind of guarantee to protect investments and, as demonstrated by three U.S. landings (1906-1909, 1912, 1917-1922), did not go unheeded. No field of activity was spared, whether it be the tobacco industry, infrastructure works, mines or public services. But again, it was sugar that led the way: in 1914, about 35% of the sugar was produced in U.S. mills located on the island, and this percentage rose to 63% in 1926. It is estimated that in 1905 over 60% of all farmland in the country belonged to U.S. citizens or corporations.

As a result, Havana was completely isolated from its economic base. The city's own natural resources were slipping from its fingers as was trade that had long been under its monopoly. Soon, there remained a single field that was within reach of the Cuban people: politics. And this became the subject of all ambitions.

Far from the true sources of power, politicians, merely puppets in the hands of

Washington, were increasingly dishonest. Corruption crept its way into all levels of government, and increasing violence soon hindered the whole process altogether.

Under these circumstances, it was no surprise that the citizens of Havana became totally disillusioned with their political institutions. And the three presidents who succeeded each other at the head of the Cuban state following the U.S. intervention in 1906, José Miguel Gomez, Mario Garcia Menocal and Alfredo Zayas, did nothing to help the situation. The discontent of Cubans was embodied in a strong opposition that became even more pressing in the 1920s when a terrible economic crisis hit the country. This period of hard times brought misery to all classes in society, but especially the working class in the capital. The number of strikes and attacks augmented, and the repression became even more forceful. The election of Gerardo Machado in 1924 would ultimately be the last straw.

Gerardo Machado, former general and vice-president of the U.S.-owned Electric Bond and Share Company, infested Havana like the black plague. The moment he became president, he instigated a wave of murders that provoked a coalition of all forces hostile to the regime. The University of Havana, transformed into a stronghold for the fight against Machado, suffered the repercussions. Occupied by the military on several occasions, then closed in 1930, it still managed to channel the people's dissatisfaction into a real national movement that eventually achieved its aims.

When Machado's police killed university director Rafael Trejo in 1930, the dictator's hours were numbered. The opposition became so strong in 1933 that the United States was compelled to manifest its displeasure with Machado. Hoping to guarantee the choice of a successor, the United States tried to negotiate the president's surrender but was cut short. A general strike and a rebellion led by a group of army officers, referred to as the "sergeants' revolution," got the best of Machado, who fled the country on August 12, 1933, leaving behind total chaos.

With the city at the very edge of a nightmare, a temporary government was established and presided over by Ramon Grau San Martin, a professor at the University of Havana. He promptly instituted a series

of progressive social mea
sures and, to the cry of
"Cuba to Cubans," unilater-
ally declared the abrogation
of the Platt Amendment. For
the first time ever, Cuban
nationalism was openly
expressed in the country's
political arena, voicing its
hostility towards U.S. interference. Needless to
say, Washington
did not approve.

For some
time al-
ready, the
United
States had
been
be-
friendin
g a sim-
ple sergeant by
the name of Fulgencio
Batista. By taking charge of
the rebel officers opposing
the Machado government,
he became Cuba's strong-
man. Sumner Wells, sent as
ambassador to Havana in
the eye of the storm, understood what made this man
tick: at the head of the
army, he had orchestrated
the temporary government
of Grau; under Washing-
ton's wing, he orchestrated
its suppression.

Outflanking

It was not difficult to con-
vince Batista. Wells merely
had to promise the uncon-
ditional support of the

United States. The benefits
would come afterwards.

From 1934 to 1940, as head
of state backed by the
army, Batista held the reins
of the government and led
a severe repression, thanks
to a string of puppet presidents. But he appeared not
to have completely re-
nounced the ideals
conveyed by San
Martin's "100
days" govern-
ment. Elected
president in
1940 with
the sup-
port of left-
wing work-
ers, he
introduced
a new con-
stitution, modeled on democratic values, that officially
put an end to the social
Revolution of the 1930s.

Nevertheless, he was de-
feated in 1944 by his old
friend Ramon Grau San
Martin who, this time, was
far from fulfilling the strong
expectations of the Cuban
people. His nationalist program fell short and wide-
spread corruption perme-
ated his government. Con-
sequently, the entire political system suffered a re-
lapse into corruption and
violence that his successor,
Prio Socarras, was unable to
quell. Batista followed this
collapse from his property
in Daytona, Florida. He

soon realized that it was time for him to return to his homeland.

Elected senator *in absentia* in 1948, Fulgencio Batista returned to the country in 1949 to prepare for the 1952 presidential elections. But sensing that they might not turn in his favour, he led a coup d'état on March 10, 1952. Overthrowing President Prio Socarras's government, he settled down, with Washington's blessing, in the presidential palace. The arrival of armoured trucks and soldiers in the capital did not encounter much protest. Many Cubans thought this would bode well for a return to peace and calm. But that was not to be the case. Under such deceptive appearances, Havana would succumb to excesses and tarnish its reputation.

In concert with the American Mafia, Batista would turn Havana into the Caribbean capital of gambling and prostitution. Thousands of tourists, mostly from Florida, flocked every year to Cuba, many arriving by the ferry that commuted between the two countries several times a week. In 1957, approximately 350,000 foreigners visited Cuba – almost as many as in 1991 – most of whom hardly left the city other than for the occasional outing to the beaches in Varadero. The city's casinos, gambling clubs and brothels (there were almost 300 at the end of the 1950s) were more than enough to satisfy a clientele in search of pleasures that were illicit in their own country.

Cuba's progressive affiliation with its northern neighbour accelerated and became almost palpable. The city began to change physically, becoming increasingly Americanized. It erected concrete high-rises, drew wide thoroughfares, named its streets using numbers and letters, remodeled the Vedado into a modern neighbourhood and erected a series of luxury hotels that would make its reputation. A complete infrastructure had to be built, and bribes would be important. Investments skyrocketed in all economic spheres, and corruption was never far behind.

Revolution

All the money lavished upon the capital, however, benefited only select groups of well-placed individuals who hastened to transfer their profits abroad. The disparity between rich and poor was staggering in Havana: over 5,000 beggars lived in the streets of the city that had the greatest

Portrait

number of Cadillacs per capita in the world. The differences between Havana and the rest of the island were even more glaring. Out in the country, people lived in huts on the ground, with no running water or electricity. Illiteracy and unemployment were widespread.

In the face of so many iniquities, Batista established increasingly repressive policies. In 1956, he introduced censorship and suspended constitutional rights, but these measures were not sufficient to stop the protest movement from turning into a full-fledged revolutionary war. Armed groups reacted increasingly aggressively to the brutal acts of the dictator's special police, the infamous military intelligence service known as the SIM. And, in 1957, the citizens of Havana were angered to learn that José Antonio Echeverría, founder and commander of the revolutionary Student Directory, had attacked the presidential palace located right in the heart of the city. He and several of his companions paid with their lives, proving that no one was safe from the backlash.

But the final stroke came from the impregnable mountains on the other end of the island, where a group of rebels, headed by a bearded giant named Fidel Castro, were holed up.

Castro became known in the days following the coup d'état in March 1952. As a young lawyer, he had exposed the illegality of the coup in court. But when faced with the court's halfheartedness in the matter, the lawyer resorted to arms and, with a small group of followers, attacked the Moncada barracks in Santiago de Cuba on July 26, 1953.

This brave attempt turned into a bloody fiasco leading to Castro's arrest and 15-year prison sentence, not to mention a notoriety that he would prove himself worthy of. Liberated in 1955 when newly elected President Batista granted him political amnesty, he fled to Mexico to plot his revenge. He returned to Cuba at the end of the following year as leader of the Movimiento 26 de Julio (M-26-7), named in memory of the 1953 onslaught. From the Sierra Maestra in southeast Cuba, he launched a vast guerilla operation that would triumph over the dictature in Havana.

Exasperated by the power cuts, the destruction of sugar harvests in addition to the decrease in tourism and its fallouts, Batista responded by launching an imposing offensive in the foothills of the Sierra Maestra in May 1958. Some 12,000 armed men, armoured trucks and planes attacked rebel positions. Nothing succeeded, and the army's defeat only served to augment the prestige of Castro, who then led his *rebeldes* towards the capital.

The entire country supported him. A general strike gave momentum to his march, and Fidel made a triumphant entry into Havana on January 8, 1959. A euphoric crowd gathered across the city upon hearing of the city's liberation and the escape of the dictator who sought refuge in San Domingo for seven days. The country had once again found its dignity... but at what cost?

Realignment

After 1959, Havana did not occupy such a prominent role in Cuban history. Government policies overcame the movement which had long favoured the capital. National development was not as unbalanced, and riches were distributed more equally.

The first days of the Revolution were the most extraordinary for the *Habaneros*. They spontaneously spread out in the city and used

axes and sticks to destroy the gambling clubs and their pernicious instruments. The buying power of city-dwellers increased substantially, thanks to a series of measures introduced by the revolutionary government, as well as to higher salaries, lower electricity and telephone costs and reduced rents. Cafés and restaurants stayed open. The city streets teemed with people night and day.

But this still wasn't enough. After the tax and tariff system was structured, the first land reform broke up the *latifundias* (large parcels of land) and put sugar production back into the hands of the Cubans. These measures troubled the United States whose vested interests were directly under attack. Given the hegemonic position of the United States, it was not surprising that the two forces had a head-on collision. In 1959, the United States controlled 80% of the public services, such as electricity and telephone, 100% of the oil refineries, all the banks, 50% of the farmlands, close to 75% of the imports and 70% of the exports, including 90% of the sugar exports. A confrontation was unavoidable.

Seeing that it had been outmaneuvered, Washington

reacted instinctively. It bet on sugar. Eisenhower hoped that removing the quotas granted to Cuba would bring the country's political classes back to their senses. But the effect was exactly the opposite. Castro responded by launching a vast nationalization program that put refineries, telephone and electricity companies, banks, railways, ports, hotels and movie theatres – in short, anything that was the least bit "American" – under Cuban jurisdiction within three months. The situation escalated. Cries of joy gave way to anxiety, and anxiety eventually gave way to determination.

In response to the state takeover of its businesses, the United States ordered an embargo on all trade with Cuba. Diplomatic relations between the two countries were severed, and a large-scale destabilization campaign instilled the fear of war in the population and peaked with the failed Bay of Pigs landing in April 1961. Crushed in less than 72 hours, the attempt to overthrow the regime only amplified the nationalistic sentiment that infused the island.

These aggressive actions reinforced the socialist character of the Cuban Revolution as well as its ties with the Union of Soviet Socialist Republics (U.S.S.R.). The two countries signed commercial agreements in which the Soviet Union promised to buy Cuban sugar and supply the island with crude oil. This was how trade was conducted between the two countries for the next 30 years. Yet there still remained the threat of military intervention. Moscow promised the new regime both material and technical support, which led to the attempted missile deployment on Cuban territory. For a few days, the entire world teetered on the brink of nuclear war.

Faced with the determination of the United States, the Soviet Union ultimately had to back down, to the great despair of Fidel Castro who, from that moment on, nourished a subdued resentment towards his defender. The fact is, Castro had counted on the confrontation. He had transformed Havana into a military camp and had prepared for the worst, convinced that the socialist revolution had to declare open warfare with the capitalistic powers. *Patria o muerte.* He was disappointed.

But the call was heard. The Revolution had not only found a protector but a patron as well. All that remained was to lay down the structure that would transform Cuba into a socialist republic.

State Socialism

"With our Revolution, we not only eradicate the exploitation of one nation by another nation but the exploitation of certain men by other men as well! We have condemned the exploitation of man by man! [...] Comrades, workers and farmers, this is the socialist and democratic Revolution of the humble, with the humble and for the humble. And for this Revolution of the humble, by the humble and for the humble, we are ready to give our lives."

It was by these words that Fidel Castro announced the socialist caricature of the Revolution to the world on April 16, 1961, during the funeral ceremony of the victims of the U.S. bombing of the Havana airport that had preceded the landing in the Bay of Pigs. That same year, he launched an extensive literacy program that had stunning results. His government then attempted to cut its ties to money by providing free state services such as public transportation, education, telephone, sports events, daycare, health care, dentist and funeral services... all graciously offered by the Revolution.

There also the began a movement to detach Cuba from its subservience to the sugar culture, which symbolized its submission to foreign interests. To reach these goals, the revolutionary government proposed two solutions: industrialization and diversification.

But this proved to be more difficult than it appeared. Firstly, the exodus of thousands of Cubans fleeing the radicalization of the Revolution deprived the state of executives, directors and managers who were vital for the elaboration and application of such programs. Secondly, the effects of the U.S. embargo were rapidly being felt. There were shortages of everything: spare parts, materials and perishable goods, to name but a few. The industry soon started to run on empty and food supplies were scarce. Rationing was imposed and lineups were beginning to form outside stores. As early as 1962, *la libreta* made sure that the population had the bare minimum.

With development at a standstill, it became necessary to return to the only industry that was capable of generating the necessary capital to restructure the economy: sugar. In 1964, Castro changed direction. An agreement with the Soviet Union promised a preferential and stable price for sugar exports, and encouraged him to launch an ambitious sugar production program. He placed the prestige of the Revolution on a mega-harvesting project, which was supposed to produce up to 10 million tons of sugar by 1970. Despite enrolling all the population, it was a fiasco. Some eight and a half million tons of sugar were produced, a record in itself, but the national spirit did not fare so well, nor did the country's economy, which was now completely dismantled by the massive effort.

An intense period of questioning followed this disappointment. Castro offered his resignation, pulled himself together, blamed overcentralization and the ineptitude of the directors for the failure of the 1970 *Zafra* and the difficulties facing the Revolution, then proposed to turn the defeat into a important victory by launching an important decentralization and popular participation movement. This effort peaked with the implementation of the System of Direction and Planification of the Economy, which left more room for market operations and the establishment of a new constitution.

Fearing a downward spiral into uncontrolled capitalism as a result of the corruption and indiscipline of the workers and peasants, the movement was quelled in 1986 by the Rectification Campaign which sought to reintroduce the initial ideals of the Revolution. But 1959 was already far away, and the flame was difficult to ignite.

Throughout all this, the Revolution did succeed in putting together a vast social program for the entire population. Free health care and education were the most notable benefits during this period. But many of the successes of Cuban socialism rested on deficient economic bases soon to be exposed by external events.

Crisis

The dismantlement of the Soviet Union in 1989 had disastrous consequences on the West Indian island. The Cuban economy literally collapsed. The very structure of its relations with Eastern-bloc countries put Cuba in an extremely vulnerable position that left no room for negotiation and subsequently led to its downfall.

In fact, after the Revolution, Havana didn't really have a choice of economic partners. The United States had so successfully cut it off from its pre-1959 market as well as from other possible markets in Latin America that the Cuban state had to cling to the Soviet Union like a drowning person hangs on to a life jacket. In merely two years, between 1959 and 1961, Cuba's exports to socialist countries increased from 2.2% to 74% of its total exports, and the imports from 0% to 70%. This tendency was maintained for nearly 30 years to such a degree that in 1986, 86% of trade was still conducted with Comecon, the common market for socialist countries which Cuba had joined in 1972.

However, trade with the Soviet Union was not very realistic. Thanks to a barely concealed subsidy, Cuba sold nickel, citrus fruits and especially sugar to the socialist bloc at prices much higher than the market dictated in return for which it received fertilizers, foodstuffs, industrial equipment and, more particularly, oil at less than market prices. This resulted in a kind of economic mirage that would finally disappear to reveal the harsh reality.

The collapse of the socialist bloc shed light on this ruse. The Cuban economy was unable to survive the loss of its traditional markets, the brutal end of its economic collaboration plans and the staggering reduction in fuel and raw material deliveries. This was followed by the dislocation of the production system and of services, as well as a sudden drop in the standard of living, reinforced by the U.S. blockade as a final *coup de grâce*.

To confront this catastrophe, on October 1, 1990, Havana introduced the "special period in peacetime." This was defined as the period of time necessary to reorient international economic relations and rebuild the national production system. It was implemented as an austerity program with serious consequences for the Cuban population, which was already crippled by the severe reduction of consumption and industrial activities, drastic power cuts and job rationalization. The State forgot its socialist ideals and streamlined its spending, increased the cost of nonessential foodstuffs, introduced taxes, instituted tariffs on goods and services that had been free until then, and encouraged the privatization of many sectors of the economy. Cuba toppled over into market socialism.

Historical Resume

1492   Christopher Columbus lands in Cuba.

1508   Sebastian de Ocampo tours the island and sees the great harbour of Havana.

1514   Havana is founded on the southern coast of the island.

1519   Havana is moved to its actual site.

1555   French corsairs destroy the city.

1556   The general harbour master's office is founded in Havana.

1564   The first great fleet departs.

1589   The city is fortified.

1607   Havana becomes the capital of the island.

1674   The walls of the old city are completed.

1700   The Bourbons ascend to the throne of Spain.

1717   The monopoly on tobacco is implemented.

1728   The University of Havana is founded.

1740   The Real Compania de Comercio is established.

1762   The British take over the city.

1789   The bishop's palace is built in Havana.

1791   Slaves revolt in Haiti.

1810   Independence wars begin on the continent.

1837   The first railway links Havana to its hinterland.

1868   The first Cuban war of independence begins.

1895	The second Cuban war of independence begins.
1898	The Hispano-American war takes place.
1899	The U.S. occupation begins.
1902	The republic of Cuba is created and the country obtains its first constitution.
1906	First military intervention of the United States.
1912	Second intervention.
1917	Third intervention.
1920	A major economic crisis hits the island.
1924	Machado is elected.
1933	Ramon Grau San Martin undertakes his "100-day" government.
1940	Batista is elected president and establishes the second constitution of the country.
1952	Military coup led by Batista.
1953	Castro attacks the Moncada barracks.
1956	Castro returns from exile in Mexico.
1959	Castro and his *rebeldes* liberate the country.
1960	Cuban nationalization program and U.S. embargo.
1961	Failed landing in Bay of Pigs.
1962	Missile crisis.
1964	Cuba signs commercial agreements with the Soviet Union.
1970	The large-scale *Zafra* fails.
1972	Cuba joins the Comecon.
1976	Third Cuban constitution.

1979	Havana hosts the summit of the non-aligned countries.
1986	The "rectification of errors and the struggle against negative tendencies" campaign is launched.
1989	The communist bloc collapses.
1990	The "special period in peacetime" begins.
1993	First measures are taken to open up the economy.
1994	Thousands of Cubans flee to the United States after the Cuban government is reinforced.
1995	The Cuban government passes a law allowing foreigners to hold 100% of shares in Cuban businesses.
1996	U.S. Congress passes the Helms-Burton law, designed to dramatically reduce foreign investments in Cuba.

Today

Measures taken to address the crises must, in the mean-time, guarantee the survival of the Revolution's social benefits. Nevertheless, such measures sow ambiguity, and many wonder whether the State will be able to survive this restructuring. It is now clear for all that if socialism brought Cubans national pride and a certain social justice, its results are far less conclusive in the realms of economy and democratization.

The Revolution played a decisive role in the country's history. It confirmed the birth of a people and its inalienable occupation of a territory, completing what was started in 1868. But the confrontation with the northern giant forced the country to close up on itself, to confine itself to a position that did not take its geographic reality into account.

The current situation is almost surreal. Old American cars put the city back into a world that no longer wishes to be on the verge of a revolution. Much of Havana's charm is due to this timeless atmosphere born out of its political convictions. The fact is, very few people can live in such austerity and Havana appears to be ready once again to take its place as a metropolis in the Caribbean.

Political System

Havana is the political hub of Cuba. Government buildings and political organizations are grouped around the Plaza de la Revolucion.

Up until 1976, the archipelago was governed by the "Fundamental Law," inspired by the 1940 constitution. That year, a new constitution was presented to the Cuban people and approved by a referendum.

Cuba then defined itself as a presidential-type socialist state. The legislative power was entirely in the hands of the National Assembly, whereas the executive power was shared by the State Council, representing the legislative organ between sessions, and the Cabinet.

At the local level, the Constitution established 169 Municipal Assemblies and 14 Provincial Assemblies.

Initially, the system anticipated that the members of the Municipal Assemblies would be elected by popular vote and that the elected would then appoint representatives for the Provincial Assemblies, who would in turn choose the deputies for the National Assembly. But in 1993, the system was simplified by allowing National Assembly delegates to be directly elected by the people. This slightly strengthened the democratic process.

Deputies of the National Assembly are elected for five-year terms. The opposition is not allowed to present any candidates, however, voters can either abstain from voting or reject the candidate inscribed on the ballot paper.

The Constitution recognizes only one political party, the Communist Party of Cuba (CPC). This only confirms the fact that the CPC has been the only legal political party in the country since 1965.

The leader of the Cuban state has a say on the complete system. The leader presides over the Cabinet and the State Council, represents the state and the government, directs general policies, supervises the operations of ministers and other administrative organisms, proposes to the National Assembly the names of people to be designated to the Cabinet, ratifies decrees, laws and other resolutions of the Council of State, and is at the head of the Armed forces of the Revolution. Fidel Castro occupies this non-elective position.

Economy

Cuba has fallen on difficult times since the early 1990s. In the wake of the decline of the Soviet Union and the Eastern bloc, the country's economy completely collapsed, forcing a profound restructuring of the very foundations of the state. Although theoretically still in search of the social ideal it gave itself in 1959, the Cuban republic now leans more and more towards capitalism. A strange amalgam of ideals and pragmatism, "market socialism" is trying to take root on this big island.

The "special period in peacetime" provoked a drastic decrease in the standard of living of Cubans, forcing the government to act promptly. Overwhelmed by the turn of events, the

State released itself from a host of services that congested its administration and no longer had the proper funding. To alleviate the most urgent needs, it allowed free employment and privatization, first in the construction and food industries, and then in many other sectors of the economy.

Shortages of all kinds made the situation even worse. The end of agreements with members of Comecon cut the country off from its sources of supply. Cuba had to look to outside markets to procure the foodstuffs necessary for its survival and pay dearly for them. The quest for dollars became the state's top priority, and the first place to get them was in the black market that had flourished for years all over Cuba. The decriminalization of the possession of greenbacks and the opening of stores that only accepted dollars severely penalized a section of the population by channeling products, often of dire necessity, to these businesses. But the dollar re-established itself in the country's economy.

This still wasn't enough. Going one step further, the Constitution (Article 16) permitted the creation of independent Cuban corporations that operated auton-

Portrait

Free Peasant Markets

Free peasant markets, or *agromercados*, began in 1980. In the wake of the decentralization and restructuring that marked the end of the 1970s, the government authorized these markets in hopes of eliminating the food shortages facing the population, especially in Havana.

State farms were initially converted into farming cooperatives. Once state quotas were reached, farmers were free to do whatever they wanted with the surplus. They were also free to set the prices and choose the crops to grow.

In 1982, the free peasant markets came under severe attack because of the abuses they caused. Exorbitant prices, excessive profits and diversion of state funds forced the government to intervene and regulate their operation. These measures obviously had little effect. In May 1986, the markets were permanently closed for the very same reasons. The corruption was so widespread that the *agromercados* became the main targets of the "rectification campaign."

It has only been since 1994, in the midst of the worst food shortage, that free peasant markets have been allowed to operate once again. There is still corruption, but what else can be done when the population must be fed? For the poorest Cubans, these markets symbolize their increasing misery and the discriminatory capitalism that is invading the socialist island.

omously, without State interference. Established in 1992, Cubanacan, Cimex and Cubalse were just a few examples of the 500-odd self-financing Cuban businesses in international trade, whose measure of success was their profitability.

In the same vein, to alleviate the lack of resources and capital and boost an economy on the brink of collapse, the country opened its doors to foreign capital. Starting in 1989, economic associations with foreign partners grew more numerous. To reassure potential investors, a decree added to Article 23 of the Constitution legitimized mixed corporations on condition that the State's portion was never less than 51%. Since then however, it appears that even this limit has been abandoned, and foreign investors in Cuba today have very few restrictions.

It was tourism that took the mixed regime to new dimensions. Cuba made tourism its main economic activity, and investments in this field reached unequalled heights and revenues of over $1 billion in 1995.

Exports remain an important part of the Cuban economy and new markets are progressively replacing those that existed before 1990. Sugar and nickel are still the two most exported products, followed by citrus fruits. Another new important source of revenue for the State is the sale of serums, vaccines and other by-products. Biotechnology and the pharmaceutical industry are in full expansion and, combined, could soon form the fourth most important source of revenue

after sugar, nickel and tourism.

The Cuban economy has improved since 1994, and Havana has been the first to profit. The port is busy again after years of stagnation, and the creation of new companies has brought the city its fair share of corporate headquarters and administrative infrastructures. Furthermore, Havana is one of eight zones targeted for large-scale touristic development, which guarantees it a substantial part of the State's investments in this field of activity. Administrative capital, tourist metropolis and top industrial centre of the country, the city is slowly rediscovering its predominant role on the island.

Population

The population of Havana is approximately 2.2 million inhabitants, close to one fifth of the archipelago's total population. Like the rest of the country, the citizens of Havana are divided into three main groups: the *Meztisos* (of mixed parentage), the *Creoles* (Creoles, or European descendants born on the island) and the *Morenos* of African heritage. Another group is the *Chinos* who came from China and the Philippines in the late 1840s to replace Black immigration once slavery became illegal. Although it would be false to say that no racism exists between the various groups, the policies of the Cuban state since the Revolution have greatly lessened the differences.

The population of Havana experienced its greatest increase during the years of the republic when thousands of peasants settled down in the capital to flee rural misery. Since the Revolution, rural exodus has virtually ended and demographic growth has stabilized, thanks in part to the State's policies on agricultural development.

Habaneros speak Spanish. There is no local dialect in Havana or in the rest of Cuba, as can be heard in Haiti or Jamaica. There is, however, a colourful way of speaking in the city which is similar to the slang heard in big North American cities.

After long being muffled, the Catholic faith is displayed more and more freely in the capital. Since the end of the 1990s, corresponding with the pope's visit in early 1998, the

Cuban government has grown more tolerant in religious matters. Havana also comprises a large population of Protestants, a remnant of the U.S. domination, as well as Afro-Cuban forms of worship.

Arts and Culture

Havana expresses its European heritage to an extent found nowhere else in the Caribbean. Its urban character lends the culture a finish that surprises and delights.

Architecture

Havana proudly displays a rich architectural legacy. It is true that many buildings were neglected during the first years of the Revolution, but things are slowly changing. Since tourism has become one of the government's major industries, aided by funds provided by

Iglesia del Espíritu Santo

UNESCO, more and more buildings in the old city are being restored. Havana's architectural development reads from east to west: Habana Vieja, Prado, Centro Habana, Vedado and Miramar, each neighbourhood faithfully reflecting a period in the city's history.

Age of Fortresses

In the first years of the colony, the city's architecture had first and foremost to fulfil military requirements. In the middle of the 16th century, a vast network of fortresses was created to surround the Caribbean Sea, and Cuba was the cornerstone. Designed by Italian military architect Juan Bautista Antonelli, the Moro and La Punta forts, built between 1589 and 1630, lent the city its martial look. Behind these massive constructions were camps, commercial warehouses, as well as *bohios*, tumbledown wooden residences.

Baroque

Midway through the 17th century, things slowly began to change in the city. As a result of the missionary influence on the colony, churches and convents popped up all over the city. This rather somber style of baroque architecture was known as *herreriano* in honour of celebrated architect Juan de Herrera whose works included, among others, the Escurial Palace in Madrid. This style gave the buildings imposing portals that reinforced the city's defensive image. These richly decorated portals were generally flanked by one or two towers. The Espiritu Santo Church, completed in 1640, is a good example of this style of architecture.

Moorish-style frieze

In the 18th century, this austere style gave way to a freer type of baroque which was more ornate, without the exuberance of Mexican baroque. The wealth of precious wood led to the creation of ceilings of great finesse in the "mudejar" style, directly inspired by the Moorish traditions of the metropolis.

The Hispano-Moorish influence was also felt in the sumptuous private homes that began to appear around the great *plazas*.

True expressions of Andalusia, these houses were built around a central courtyard, called *patio*, with colonnades and covered balconies to protect from the sun, red-tiled roofs and colourful earthenware decorations called *azulejos*.

This period also gave birth to most of the government buildings in the old city. The Palacio del Secundo Cabo and the Palacio de los Capitanes Generales, both in front of the Plazas de Armas, were built in a similar style in the second half of the 18th century.

Neoclassicism and Art Nouveau

Following in the footsteps of Europe, Havana embraced neoclassicism at the turn of the 19th century. Inspired by the models of antiquity, lines straightened out and facades became more refined. This new, clean-cut urbanism was more organized. All along the Paseo del Prado and around Parque Central, the new heart of the city, Cuban neoclassicism works of art were erected.

In answer to the sugar economy and its expansion, most of the new constructions were destined for commercial and industrial uses. The Palacio de Aldama, one of the first examples of neoclassicism in Havana completed in the 1840s, the Manzana de Gomez, a large store built in 1910 in front of Parque Centre and the Hotel Inglaterra, dating back to 1875, are some of the most beautiful illustrations of this style.

Bits of art nouveau were added to neoclassicism in the early 20th century. The Gran Teatro, jewel of the Prado, is an admirable combination of styles and contributed to making art nouveau an underlying artistic basis for the eclecticism that defined 20th-century architecture.

Modernism

With the arrival of the United States in the early 20th century, the city moved even closer to the west. The construction of the Malecón, the pride of the city, allowed urban development to avoid Centro Habana, which would likely have accommodated the population overflow from around the bay. Wealthy Americans and Cubans settled down near La Rampa, the new fashionable avenue. The Vedado was covered in traditional colonial-style residences that were adapted to North American standards of living by adding elements of art nouveau, Art Deco and even the Santa Fe style from the U.S. southwest. This trend also extended to the posh Miramar neighbourhood.

The first skyscrapers appeared in the 1940s and 1950s. These ironclad structures, devoid of decorative elements, posed as symbols of modernity. The Hotel Habana Libre, formerly the Hilton, and the Hotel Riviera, crown jewel of the gambling empire owned by the notorious gangster Meyer Lansky, illustrate the importance of tourism in Havana.

Revolutionary Architecture

The Revolution was forced to deal with an urgent housing shortage. The architectural style of this period was pragmatic above all. In the city's suburbs and on the other side of the bay, its aestheticism rarely went beyond a block of cement with windows. There were a few exceptions, however, such as the Instituto Superior de Arte's faculty of visual arts that was built in Miramar in 1961.

Literature

Cuban literature plays an important role in Spanish culture. In its first years, Cuban literature was particularly influenced by the Creole charm of its interior. It became progressively more urban though, especially in the 1950s.

It is impossible to speak of Cuban literature without mentioning Cirilo Villaverde and his famous *Cecilia Valdés*. This novel is the basis of all Cuban literary knowledge. It also provides an unsurpassed portrayal of Havana in the first half of the 19th century. The streets, monuments and buildings it describes evoke the city in its hours of glory.

Recognized as an important literary figure in the Cuban archipelago, Alejo Carpentier died in 1980 while working as an advisor at the Cuban Embassy in Paris. His great literary works, some of which depict Havana, earned him the Cervantes prize. Published in 1978, his last novel, *La Consagración de la Primavera*, covers the period from Machado to the Bay of Pigs landing and describes Havana through the eyes of a Russian ballerina and her architect husband. This last characteristic adds a particularly interesting dimension to the book for those who are interested in the city's architecture. Published in 1962, *El Siglo de las Luces* (*Explosion in a Cathedral*) examines the early 19th century and the impact of the Haitian rebellion on the Havana mentality.

From the same generation, José Lezama Lima also wrote about Havana in works such as *Paradiso*, which was published in 1966. Not as accessible, this novel tackles the city in a less blatant fashion than Carpentier, giving his characters a more profound dimension.

Exile literature provides gripping portraits of Havana. Guillermo Cabrera Infante clearly distinguishes himself in this realm. In his 1965 work entitled *Tres Tristes Tigres* (*Three Trapped Tigers*), he uses humour and cynicism to describe the nightlife in the Cuban capital right before the Revolution. In 1970, this book won the well-deserved best foreign novel prize in Paris. *La Habana para un Infante Difunto* (*Infante's Inferno*) covers a longer period, from the 1940s to the 1950s. This novel was written and published in London in 1978, while the author was in exile. In the 1950s, he also wrote a series of short stories published in 1962 under the title *Así en la Paz*

como en la Guerra (*Writes of Passage*) in which he profiles the ubiquitous gangsterism in the capital during this period.

Reinaldo Arenas, a poet exiled because of his open opposition to the *Comandante* regime, writes about the marginal and the dissatisfied living in Castro's Havana. His autobiography, *Antes que Anochezca* (*Before Night Falls*), describes his life experiences and provides a new perspective on the Cuban Revolution. He also wrote *Viaje a La Habana*, which is composed of three stories about the city and was published in 1990.

Finally, from another generation, Zoé Zaldez published *La Nada Cotidiana* in 1995, a beautiful novel about the difficulties of life in Havana during the "special period in peacetime."

Movies

Cuban cinema really took off in 1959 with the creation of the Instituto Cubano de Arte y Industria Cinematografica (ICAIC). Fruit of the Revolution, this institute was socially committed from the start, causing it to focus mainly on documentaries. This tendency even affected popular cinema, and docudramas

Portrait

were a major part of the ICAIC's film production.

Havana is at the heart of the work of Tomas Gutiérrez Alea. Before his death in 1996, he was able to draw a discriminating portrait of this incomparable city through 10 or so feature films. His 1968 masterpiece (for many, the masterpiece of all Cuban cinema), *Memorias del Subdesarrollo* (*Memories of Underdevelopment*) examines the life of a lower-class man in Havana after the Revolution who, upon witnessing the collapse of a world for which he had no sympathy, already feels excluded from the one that replaces it. The persistent mentality of the lower and middle classes in the first years of the Revolution is a major theme in his films.

Among his other noteworthy movies, *Hasta Cierto Punto* (1983) projects images of Havana's port and the life around it and *Fresa y Chocolate* (*Strawberries and Chocolate*), co-directed by Juan Carlos Tabio and screened in 1994, will especially delight those who are interested in Havana and its culture. This film denunciates the intolerance of the Castro regime in the late 1970s, while using striking imagery to portray the Cuban capital.

After Alea's death, very few films can claim to provide a sensitive presentation of the reality in which *Habaneros* live. That being said, two film-makers distinguish themselves: Sara Gomez whose 1974 film *De Cierta Manera* recounts the trials and tribulations of the residents of a new neighbourhood in Havana, and Juan Carlos Tabio, mentioned above, who explores the phenomenon of apartment-trading in the capital in his 1983 film *Se Permuta*.

Havana is one of the most important film-making centres in Latin America. Since 1979, it has been hosting the Festival of New Latino-American Cinema in the month of December.

Music

Havana was not the birthplace of such quintessential Cuban rhythms as the rumba, *danzon*, *son* and bolero, which were conceived far from the capital. Havana was more of a melting pot in which these types of music were revived and enriched by foreign influences. The city was also a renowned place for talented musicians to gather as early as the 1920s, largely to satisfy the demands of the blossoming tourism industry.

For instance, the eminently Cuban sounds of *son* were first heard in Havana during this period with groups like the Sexteto Habanero, the Septeto Nacional and the Trio Matamoros. *Son* borrowed the techniques and brass section from jazz while maintaining its own unique rhythm. Recording contracts between a number of groups and big U.S. companies quickened the popularity of the genre.

Nowadays, Havana pulses to the beats of Latin jazz and *salsa*, which both combine jazz and Afro-Cuban music. But it is the latter that dominates the city's music scene by far. Along with New York and San Juan de Puerto Rico, Havana is a major capital of *salsa* its rhythms being similar to *son*. A more spirited and vigorous version of *salsa* known as *songo* now exists as well. Havana abounds in popular orchestras specializing in this musical genre.

Last but not least, we must mention the lauded movie, *Buena Vista Social Club*, directed by Wim Wenders, in which illustrious performers revive the Cuban music which lulled Havana during the years of the Republic.

Thanks to American Ry Cooder, a group of retired golden-aged Cuban musicians climbed back up on stage to offer the world a series recordings and shows that became wildly popular. Acclaimed German director Wim Wenders even filmed a documentary about the band, which he named after it.

Royal palm

Table of Distances (km/mi)

Via the Shortest Route

1 mile = 1.62 kilometres
1 kilometre = 0.62 miles

	Camagüey	Cienfuegos	Guantánamo	Holguín	Havana	Matanzas	Pinar del Río	Sancti Spíritus	Santa Clara	Varadero
Baracoa	431/267	873/541	115/71	224/139	1080/670	1018/631	1240/769	728/451	808/501	1020/632
Camagüey		327/203	431/267	207/128	534/331	272/169	694/430	182/113	262/162	474/294
Cienfuegos			758/470	534/331	251/156	200/124	411/255	145/90	65/40	202/125
Guantánamo				224/139	965/598	903/560	1125/698	613/380	693/430	905/561
Holguín					741/459	679/421	901/559	389/241	469/291	681/422
Havana						102/63	160/99	352/218	272/169	144/89
Matanzas							262/162	290/180	210/130	42/26
Pinar del Río								512/317	432/268	304/188
Sancti Spíritus									80/50	292/181
Santa Clara										212/131

Example: the distance between Pinar del Río and Cienfuegos is 411km or 255mi.

© ULYSSES

Practical Information

This chapter will help you plan your trip to Havana.

It includes general information and practical advice designed to familiarize you with local customs.

All prices quoted in this guide are in US dollars.

Entrance Formalities

Make sure you bring all the necessary papers to enter and exit the country. Though requirements are not very strict, certain documents are required to travel in Cuba, so keep them in a safe place.

Passport

To travel in Cuba, visitors must have a passport in their possession at all times. The passport must be valid for the full length of the stay. Travellers from the United States are allowed to travel in Cuba and must have a valid passport to do so. See the section for American travellers below.

It is a good idea to keep a photocopy of the key pages of your passport, and to write down your passport number and its expiry date. This will make it much easier to replace your passport in the eventuality that it is lost or stolen. If this should occur, contact your country's consulate or embassy (see addresses below) to have a new one issued.

Tourist Card

Foreign visitors to Cuba are also required to have a tourist permit *(tarjeta de turista)*. In Canada, the tourist permit is included in the price of vacation packages. If you pay only the airfare to Cuba, you must pay an additional $20US for a tourist permit. If you are arriving from another country, consult your travel agent about purchasing this permit.

The *tarjeta de turista* allows visitors to stay in the country for the entire duration of their trip. Be careful not to lose it since it must be returned to authorities at the end of the trip.

Cuban regulations require you to have reserved a hotel room for at least two nights upon your arrival. If you do not do this, the immigration officers may delay your entry and even choose a hotel room for you, regardless of the price. If you have not already made a hotel reservation or if you are staying with a family, write the name of a well-known hotel on your tourist permit. This way, you can avoid potential problems.

American Travellers

American travellers are allowed to visit Cuba, and are usually treated well by authorities and the population in general. There are, however, no flights from the United States to Cuba; visitors must therefore purchase their tickets and make a stopover in Mexico or Canada. Americans who have been in Cuba may have difficulty returning to the United States. For this reason Cuban customs officers will not stamp your passport if you don't want them to. There is a disadvantage, however; U.S. consular authorities will not be able to help you while you're in Cuba. You will have to visit either the Canadian or Mexican embassy.

Airport Departure Tax

Each person leaving Cuba must pay a departure tax of $20 US. The tax is collected at the airport when you check in for your return flight. Remember to keep this amount in cash, as credit cards are not accepted.

Customs

Visitors may enter the country with up to one litre of alcohol, 200 cigarettes and up to $100 US worth of goods (not counting personal belongings). Bringing in illegal drugs and firearms is, of course, prohibited.

Embassies and Consulates

Embassies and consulates can be an invaluable source of help to visitors who find themselves in trouble. For example, consulates can provide names of doctors or lawyers in the case of death or serious injury. However, only urgent cases are handled. It should also be noted that any cost resulting from these services is not absorbed by the consulates.

BELGIUM
Avenida 5 no. 7408
at the corner of Calle 76
Miramar
☎24-2410 or 24-2561

CANADA
Calle 30 no. 518
at the corner of Avenida 7
Miramar
☎24-2517

GERMANY
Calle B no. 652, Esq. A 13
Vedado
☎33-2539 or 33-2569
≈33-1586

GREAT BRITAIN
Calle 34 no. 708, between Calles 7 and 17
Miramar
☎24-1771 or 24-1772

ITALY
Calle Paseo no. 606, between Calle 25 and 27
Vedado
☎33-3334 or 33-3356

NETHERLANDS
Calle 8 no. 307, between Avenida 3 and 5
Miramar
☎24-2511 or 24-2512

SPAIN
Calle Cárcel no. 51, at the corner of Calle Zulueta
Habana Vieja
☎33-8025 or 33-8026

SWITZERLAND
Avenida 5 no. 2005
Miramar
☎24-2611 or 24-2729

Calzada between Calle L and M
Vedado
☎30-0551 or 33-3550

UNITED STATES
There is a U.S. Interests Section at the Swiss Embassy.

Cuban Embassies and Consulates Abroad

These offices emit the necessary visas, for business trips for example, and usually also house a tourist office of sorts in order to assist travellers to prepare their trip to Cuba. Staff here answer questions and give out brochures.

CANADA
Cuban Embassy
388 Main St.
Ottawa, Ontario K1S 1E3
☎ *(613) 563-0141*
= *(613) 563-0068*

Cuban Consulate
1415 avenue des Pins Ouest
Montréal, Québec H3B 1B2
☎ *(514) 843-8897*

Cuban Consulate
5353 Dundas W., Kipling Square,
Suite 401
Toronto, Ontario M9B 6H8
☎ *(416) 234-8181*
= *(416) 234-2754*

BELGIUM
Cuban Embassy
77 rue Robert-Jones
1180 Bruxelles
☎ *343-0020*
= *344-9691*

GREAT BRITAIN
Cuban Consulate
15 Grape St.
London WC1V 6P4
☎ *240-2488*

ITALY
Cuban Embassy
Via Licinia, 7
00153 Roma
☎ *396-575-5984*
= *396-574-5445*

SPAIN
Cuban Embassy
Paseo de la Habana, 194
between Calle de la Mcarena and
Rodrigues Binilla
Madrid
☎ *341-359-2500*
= *341-359-6385*

Switzerland
Cuban Embassy
Seminarstr 29
3006 Berne
☎ *4131-302-2115*
= *4131-302-2111*

UNITED STATES
Cuban Interest Section
2630 16th Street NW
Washington, D.C., 20009
☎ *(202) 797-8518 or 797-8609*
= *(202) 797-8521 or 986-7283*

Tourist Information

Infotur, the Havana tourist bureau, has an office at the airport, as well as in the old quarter of Havana *(Obispo 358)* and in Miramar *(5ta. Ave. Esq.A112)*. In addition to getting tourist information, you can also make reservations for excursions and buy bus tickets here.

Cubatur
Calle F no.157, between Calle 9 and
Calzada
Vedado
☎33-4155
⇌33-3529
This agency specializes in
group and private tours.

Havanatur
Calle 2 no. 17, between 1 and 2
Miramar
☎33-2273
⇌33-2877
Havanatur offers more or
less the same services as
Cubatur.

Casa de la Amistad
Paseo no. 646
between Calles 17 and 19
☎33-3544
⇌33-3515
This old colonial residence
houses a competitively
priced hotel-reservation
service for the whole country. You can also sign up
for interesting cultural excursions here.

Tour Operators and Travel Agencies

Caribe Sol
Calle 2 no. 17
between Calle no. 1 and
Calle no. 2
Miramar
☎24-2161

Havanatur
Calle 2 no. 17
between Calle no. 1 and Calle no. 3
Miramar
☎24-2161
⇌24-2877

Hola Sun
Calle 2 no. 17
between Calle no. 1 and Calle no. 2
Miramar
☎24-2273
⇌24-2877

Tourist Offices Abroad

CANADA
Toronto
55 Queen St. E. #705
Toronto, ON, M5C 1R6
☎(416) 362-0700
⇌(416) 362-6799

Montréal
440 Boul. René Levesque Ouest, #1402
Montreal, QC, H2Z 1U7
☎(514) 875-8004

ITALY
Via G. Fara, 30
20124 Milano
☎39 2 66981463
⇌39 2 6690042

Getting There

By Plane

Aeropuerto Internacional José-Martí

Located 15km (9.3mi) from Havana, ☎33-5177, 5178 or 5179.

The airport in Havana is sizeable and full-serviced. It does not, however have a good selection of boutiques, and not surprisingly, the shopping is more expensive here than it is in the cities. Taxis can bring travellers into the city. The taxis are metered, so there is no price negotiation, even for long distances. Generally there are no buses at the airports, except those chartered by wholesalers for travellers with reservations.

All of the car rental companies have small counters at the airports, so you can rent a car as soon as you arrive. They are all located one next to one another, so be sure to compare rates.

Transferts to La Havana: Taxis wait outside the various exits of the Aeropuerto José-Martí, located 15km (9.3mi) from the city on Avenida Rancho Boyeros. It costs between $15 and $20 to get downtown or to Old Havana. If you're on a tight budget, opt for the **Panataxi** company, whose rates are by far the lowest. Otherwise, you can wait for one of the public buses on Avenida Boyeros or simply stick out your thumb; hitchhiking is very common in Cuba. With a little luck, you'll get to ride in an old American car from the 1950s and you'll immediately find yourself immersed in the picturesque world of Havana.

International Flights:
You will be charged a $20 departure tax when you check in at the airport for your return flight. This tax must be paid in cash.

Terminals: The Aeropuerto José-Martí has three terminals. The first two are located side by side in the same building. The third is used for Aerocaribbean and Aerotaxi flights to various tourist destinations, including Cayo Largo and Isla de la Juventud.

Airlines

Aerocaribbean
Calle 23, at the corner of Calle P
Vedado
☎*33-4543*
≈*33-5016*

Aerotaxi
Calle 27 no.102, at the corner of
Calle N
Vedado
☎ *32-8127*
⇆ *32-8121*

Aeroflot
Mon to Fri 8:30am to 4pm
Sat 8am to noon
Calle 23 no. 64
☎ *33-3200 or 33-3759*
⇆ *33-3288*

Air Canada
Mon to Sat 8am to 7pm
José Martí
☎ *74-9111 or 74-9116*

AOM
La Rampa – Calle 23
at the corner Avenida P
Vedado

Cubana de Aviación
Calle 2 no. 64
☎ *33-4949*
⇆ *33-4950*

Iberia
Mon to Fri 9am to 4pm
Sat 9am to noon
Calle 23 no. 74
☎ *33-5041 or 33-5042*
⇆ *33-2751*

KLM-Royal Dutch Airlines
Calle 23 no. 64
☎ *33-3730*
⇆ *33-3729*

LTU
Calle 23 no. 64
☎ *33-3254 or 33-3525*
⇆ *33-2789*

Mexicana
Calle 23 no. 74
☎ *33-3531, 33-3532 or 33-3533*
⇆ *33-3077*

TAAG
Calle 23 no. 64
at the corner of Infanta
☎ *33-2527*
⇆ *33-3049*

Viasa
Calle L, at the corner of Calle 23
Hotel Habana Libre Tryp
☎ *33-3130*
⇆ *33-3611*

Finding Your Way Around

By Bus

The Cuban tour operator Rumbos now runs a tour bus for visitors, the Vaivén. Its long route from the Palacio de las Convenciones to the Morro Cabaña passes the Plaza de la Revolución and the Malecón.

For $4 you can buy a day pass and use the bus as much as you wish. It runs every day from morning until 9pm.

Aside from this bus, Havana's public bus service is a real nightmare. There are no printed schedules or maps of bus routes. The best way to take the bus is to go to one of the numerous stops and tell someone waiting there where you're trying to go. Travelling during rush hour requires a lot of patience, and the long lines are sure to discourage even the most determined tourists from using this means of transportation. The bus is very cheap (one to three pesos), however, and if you spend a few days in Havana, you should try to take it at least once; it's a colourful experience. Known as *camellos* (camels), the long, overcrowded trailer trucks are a perfect example of the city's public transportation crisis.

The most useful routes are probably those that go from Old Havana to the Vedado. These are buses no. 195, 232, 264 and 298. In Old Havana, take them at Parque de la Fraternidad; in the Vedado, it is easiest to go to Parque Coppelia, on the La Rampa side.

By Taxi

There are many taxi companies to help you get around. However, their taxis are rarely parked in front of hotels or other places frequented by tourists, so you'll have to telephone for one.

Panataxi (☎55-5555) has a large fleet of Ladas and offers the best rates in town.

Turistaxi (☎33-5539) has the best cars, and its drivers usually park at hotel entrances.

All tourist taxis have meters, and the rates are not negotiable, even for long trips. For example, there is no fixed rate for a trip from the airport to downtown Havana (usually about $15), or from Havana to Varadero.

Local Taxis

Since January 1996, scores of taxi permits have been issued in Havana, following the recent easing of restrictions on private and family enterprises. These cars roam the streets of Havana with a cardboard sign reading "taxi" in their windshield. The rates are determined by the driver, but you should never pay more than $1 for a trip within the city, or $5 per hour.

If you choose this kind of transportation, try and stop one of the old American cars that travel through the city on predetermined routes. The price is fixed and is paid in pesos. You will be sharing the car with a variable number of Cubans. To travel from Old Havana to the Vedado or

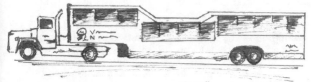

Camello

Miramar, try finding one on Calle San Lázaro at the corner of the Prado or on Avenida Simón Bolívar at the corner of Parque Central. In the Vedado, go to the corner of La Rampa and Calle O.

Particulares

Many underpayed Cuban professionals have abandoned their jobs to become black-market taxi drivers. They park in front of the most touristy places in town. You can use their services for just one trip or hire a driver for an entire day. These "taxis" are very useful, and are in great demand for trips outside of the city, since they can make an excursion to the beach much more affordable. To get to the Playas del Este (eastern beaches), for example, you can go to the Estación de Trenes (train station), where you'll find drivers ready to chauffeur you about.

Cubans are usually charged between $1 and $2 per person for a trip to the beach in Santa Maria. Ten dollars for a full car is the minimum a foreigner can hope to pay, however. If you are planning to spend the afternoon at the beach and would like the driver to wait for you, $15 is sufficient ($20 to $30 for the day). If you want to make an inexpensive trip outside the city, this is definitely your best option.

By Car

Driving

Driving in Havana is no more complicated than in any other big city in the world. You do, however, have to get used to sharing the streets with thousands of cyclists and remember that bicycles always have the right of way over cars. For example, if you are at an intersection and you have to turn right, wait until all the cyclists have passed; they will rarely stop to let you go by. Cyclists are unpredictable: they generally pay little heed to the rules of the road, so be careful, especially at night.

Practical Information

They will often take up an entire lane of a large avenue, and even ride right in the middle of the road as if they had every right to be there. Always pay attention to what's happening around you and be prepared to react to any situation that might arise.

Parking

Parking spots are not hard to come by in Havana. In many places, self-appointed "parking attendants" wait by the side of the road. They will offer to wash your car and keep an eye on it during your absence. It is customary to give them some change when you return. Another option is to leave your car in the parking lot of a nearby hotel.

Car Rentals

A number of companies rent cars at rates ranging from $50 to $70 per day. **Havanautos** *(Calle 36 no. 505, between Avenidas 5 and 5A, Miramar, ☎24-0647)* has branches in many hotels in Havana, as well as at the Aeropuerto José-Martí *(☎42-2175)*. The company **Transautos** also has branches in many of the city's hotels and in terminals 1 and 2 at the airport *(☎33-5177 to 79)*.

Taking into account the growth of tourism and the rigidity of the Cuban economic system, there is frequently a shortage of rental cars. To avoid inconveniences, it is often easier and more economical to rent a car when you buy your plane ticket.

Another interesting option, particularly if you do not go far from Havana, is to hire a car with a driver for the day *(about $20 to $30, see the "taxis particulares" section above)*.

By Bicycle

You can rent bicycles and motorbikes to tour the city but prices are relatively expensive if you go through accredited companies. The best way to rent a bicycle is to make arrangements directly with Cubans themselves. This is easy if you are staying at a *casa particular*, but more difficult otherwise. Try the Rumbos company, a Havana tourism specialist. Rumbos has several locations so call the central office *(☎33-3259)* to find out which one is the most convenient. A bicycle costs about $1 an hour and a motorbike $3 after paying $10 for the first hour. In both cases you can get a better deal if you rent for longer periods of time.

If you rent a bicycle, you will see that there are

scores of bicycle parking lots, or *parqueos*, in Havana, and you'll have no trouble finding one near any place you visit. The rates vary between one and two pesos per bicycle, and you usually have to pay when you leave. Make sure to lock your bike when you leave it in a *parqueo*. As all the bikes look pretty much the same, the attendant will have a hard time knowing which one is yours. For identification purposes, you will likely be given two little numbered plates; attach one to your bike and keep the other one with you. To pick up your bike, you need only show the two matching plates. These *parqueos* are a much safer alternative to leaving your bicycle on the street, even if it is locked. An unattended bicycle may well end up stripped of its wheels, pedals, handlebars and seat, since all of these parts are highly coveted in Havana.

Hitchhiking

Foreign visitors might be surprised to discover how common hitchhiking is in Havana. In response to the city's transportation problems, car pooling has become popular and sometimes even mandatory. On some license plates, you'll see the word *Estado*. The drivers of these cars, which belong to State-owned companies, are required to stop for hitchhikers and ask them which way they're going – provided of course, that there is room for them. If the driver is going in the same direction you are, hop in! The best way to stop these cars is to stand at an intersection monitored by an official in a yellow uniform. Commonly known as *amarillos*, these law enforcers flag down State-owned cars with empty seats.

Cars with the word *particular* on their license plates are privately owned. Some drivers will stop for hitchhikers, but will usually charge tourists a few dollars. Make sure to negotiate a fixed rate before getting in the car. A word of advice: offer the driver at least half what he asks for and never pay more than $5 for a trip inside city limits or more than $10 to go to the suburbs.

All in all, hitchhiking is an excellent way to get around Havana, and you're likely to make some interesting acquaintances at the same time. It is as common to see women hitchhiking as men.

Insurance

Cancellation

Travel agents generally offer you cancellation insurance when you buy your airline ticket or vacation package. This insurance allows you to be reimbursed for the ticket or package deal if your trip must be cancelled due to serious illness or death. It is up to you to weigh the cost of this insurance against the likelihood that you will require it.

Theft

Most residential insurance policies protect some of your goods from theft, even if the theft occurs in a foreign country. To make a claim, you must fill out a police report. Usually the coverage for a theft abroad is 10% of your total coverage. It may not be necessary to take out further insurance, depending on the amount covered by your current policy. As policies vary considerably, you are advised to check with your insurance company. European visitors should take out baggage insurance.

Health

This is the most useful kind of insurance for travellers, and should be purchased before your departure. Your insurance plan should be as complete as possible because health-care costs add up quickly, even in Cuba. When buying insurance, make sure it covers all types of medical costs, such as hospitalization, nursing services and doctor's fees. Make sure your limit is high enough, as these expenses can be costly. A repatriation clause is also vital in case the required care is not available on site. Furthermore, since you may have to pay immediately, check your policy to see what provisions it includes in such a situation. To avoid any problems during your vacation, always keep proof of your insurance policy on you.

Health

Cuba is a wonderful place to explore, and you can do so without having to worry about tropical diseases since most of these illnesses, including malaria, typhoid, diphtheria, tetanus, polio and hepatitis A have been eradicated from the country. No vaccinations are required to enter the country. It is nevertheless a

In Old Havana, magnificent architecture
and reminders of daily life exist side by side. - *P. Escudero*

The Palacio del Centro Gallego, which houses the Gran Teatro de La Habana, offers its angel to the skies. - *P. Escudero*

good idea to visit a traveller's clinic before leaving for advice on what precautions to take.

Illnesses

Diphtheria and Tetanus

Most people have been vaccinated against these potentially serious diseases as children. Before leaving home, however, make sure you were in fact inoculated; a booster shot may be needed. Diphtheria is a bacterial infection that is spread by secretions from the nose and throat or skin lesions of infected persons. Its symptoms include sore throat, high fever, lethargy and, on occasion, skin infections. Tetanus is also caused by a bacteria. Infection occurs when a cut in the skin comes in contact with contaminated matter (dirt or dust).

Ciguatera

This illness is caused by the ingestion of ciguatoxin, a toxin found in contaminated fish (infected by feeding on seaweed growing on coral reefs). Among the fish that become contaminated are the red snapper (*huachinango* in Spanish) and grouper. The toxin is tasteless and odourless and

resists cooking. The only way to avoid it, therefore, is not to eat these fish. Symptoms can appear quickly, sometimes only minutes after ingesting the toxin, or up to 30 hours later. They include nausea, vomiting and diarrhoea, as well as neurological symptoms like muscular aches, fatigue and an inability to tell hot from cold. There is no cure for this illness, but the symptoms can be treated.

Other Health Precautions

Bodies of fresh water are frequently contaminated by the bacteria that causes schistosomiasis. This illness, caused by a worm-like parasite that enters the body and attacks the liver and nervous system, is difficult to treat. Swimming in fresh water should thus be avoided.

Remember that consuming too much alcohol, particularly when accompanied by prolonged exposure to the sun, can cause severe dehydration.

Despite a lack of financial resources, Cuban medical facilities are on a par with North American and European standards. Medical clinics outside the big cities may appear modest, but they usually have all the necessary equipment. Medical care is free for Cubans; foreigners, however, must pay for these services in U.S. dollars. In tourist areas, there is usually an English-speaking doctor. Before a blood transfusion, be sure (when possible) that quality control tests have been carried out on the blood.

The quality of Cuba's tap-water is generally quite good, and can be drunk throughout the country. However, to avoid possible upset stomach, drink bottled water. When buying bottled water, whether in a restaurant or store, always make sure that the bottle is properly sealed. Water is normally treated in the big hotels, but check with the staff first. Raw fruit and vegetables washed in tap water (those not peeled before eating) may cause the same symptoms.

If you do get diarrhoea, there are several ways to treat it. First, try to soothe your stomach by avoiding solids; instead, drink carbonated beverages, bottled water, or weak tea or coffee (avoid milk) until you recover. As the resulting dehydration can be dangerous, drinking sufficient quantities of liquid is crucial. To remedy severe dehydration, a solution containing a litre of water, two or three teaspoons of

salt and one teaspoon of sugar will help re-establish the body's fluid balance. Pharmacies also sell ready-made preparations to help cure dehydration. Finally, gradually reintroduce solids to your system by eating easily digestible foods. Medication, such as Imodium or Pepto-Bismol, can help control intestinal discomfort. If more serious symptoms develop (high fever, intense diarrhoea), a visit to a doctor and antibiotics may be necessary.

Food and climate can also cause or aggravate various illnesses. Make sure that the food you eat is fresh (especially fish and meat) and that the food preparation area is clean. Proper hygiene, such as washing hands frequently, will help prevent you from catching something.

Walking around with bare feet is also to be avoided, as parasites and tiny insects can get into your skin and cause a variety of problems, including dermatitis and fungal infections.

Insects

Insects, which are numerous throughout the country, can be a real nuisance. They are particularly abundant during the rainy season. To avoid getting bitten or stung, cover up well, avoid brightly coloured clothing, do not wear perfume and use a good insect repellent, (minimum 35% DEET). Remember that insects are more active at sundown. When walking in the mountains or in wooded areas, wear socks and shoes that protect both feet and legs. It is also wise to bring some ointments to soothe the itching in case you do get bitten. Insect coils will allow you to enjoy more pleasant evenings on the terrace or in your room with the windows open.

The Sun

Despite its benefits, the sun causes several problems. Always bring a sunscreen (SPF 15 for adults and 25 for children) that protects against the sun's harmful rays, and apply it 20 to 30 minutes before exposure. Over-exposure can cause sunstroke (fainting, vomiting, fever, etc.), especially the first few days, as your body is getting used to the change in temperature. It is important to cover up and avoid prolonged exposure while you get used to the sun. Sunglasses and a hat will also help protect against the harmful effects of the sun.

First-Aid Kit

A small first-aid kit can help you avoid many discomforts; prepare it carefully before leaving home. Ensure that you have enough of all your regular medications, as well as a valid prescription in case you lose this supply. It can be very difficult to find certain medications in smaller Cuban towns. Other medication, including anti-malaria pills and Imodium or Pepto-Bismol, should also be bought before leaving. In addition, bring adhesive bandages, scissors, aspirin, disinfectants, analgesics, antihistamines, an extra pair of glasses, contact lens solution, and pills for upset stomach.

Emergencies

If you have the misfortune of falling ill during your stay in Havana, you need not worry, as the local hospitals generally provide fast, excellent care. The best hospitals and clinics are open to tourists. Payments are made in U.S. dollars; the medical centres have agreements with the major international insurance companies.

Practical Information

Hospital Hermanos Ameijeiras
Calle San Lázaro no. 701
between Calle Marqués González and
Calle Belascoaín
Centro Habana
☎*70-7721 to 29 or 79-8531 to 39*
⇌*33-5036*
The biggest hospital in Havana.

Hospital Comandante Manuel Fajardo
Calle Zapata, at the corner of Calle D
Vedado
☎*33-8022 or 32-2477*
⇌*33-3120*

Clínica Central Cira García
Calle 20 no. 4101, at the corner of 43
Miramar
☎*24-2811 to 144*
⇌*24-1633*

Pharmacies

All the hospitals and clinics
mentioned above offer
pharmaceutical services.
Although there is sometimes a shortage of drugs
due to the U.S. embargo
and the country's economic
problems, medical centres
and large hotels can provide tourists with medication. You can also go to the
Farmacia Internacional
*(Avenida 41, at the corner of
Calle 20, Miramar,*
☎*24-2051).*

Opticians

Óptica Miramar
Calle 4, corner of Calle 24
Miramar
☎*24-2990*
⇌*24-2893*
Óptica Miramar is an excellent optician's shop with a
prime location in Miramar.

Safety

Havana is a relatively safe
city. However, the increase
in tourism and the economic crisis have led to a
rise in crime. It is best to
keep your personal belongings with you at all times
and to be doubly careful in
areas where tourists don't
usually go. Pickpocketers
have reportedly been targeting people on the Malecón
and in the busiest parts of
Old Havana. Fortunately,
the police have started
monitoring these areas
much more carefully.

You will constantly be approached by people trying
to sell you various products,
exchange your dollars for
pesos, or accompany you.
Most of those in the tourist
areas are "professionals,"
whose sole aim is to extract
as much money from you
as possible. At best, they'll
try to get you to buy them a
beer or two. These *jineteros*
and *jineteras* (escorts) seem

friendly at first, and are not usually dangerous. However, if you choose to trust them with your personal belongings unattended, even if only for a few moments, you can easily get robbed. The more stylish the person is (jeans, walkman, gold chains, brand-name sunglasses, etc.), the more likely it is you're dealing with a true "professional."

There is no magic solution for escaping quickly when someone like this approaches you. You can, however, try saying immediately: *No tengo guaniquiqui, amigo!* (I don't have any money, my friend). *Guaniquiqui* is a term made popular by a salsa, so you'll make the person smile while at the same time stating your position clearly. In any case, it is best not to give anything at all to people who come up to you; otherwise, you might end up surrounded by a whole mob. At most, carry a supply of candies or pens to give to children.

Prostitution

Prostitution, which is increasing as fast as tourism, has taken on new meaning in Cuba. Subtlety is the key here — these men and women don't consider themselves prostitutes. In Cuba, prostitution is known as *"jineterismo"* and applies to young men and women who offer up their admiration to unsuspecting tourists in exchange for as much money and as many gifts as they can get. These very subtle characters act as gallant hosts to fool you. Unlike a prostitute, the ultimate goal of a *jinetero* or *jinetera* is to marry his or her conquest in order to leave the country. These people are generally not dangerous, though theft is common as soon as any personal objects belonging to an unsuspecting tourist are left unattended. *Jineteros* are easy to spot by their clothes: the women wear risqué, chic clothing, while the men wear expensive sunglasses, jeans and baseball caps. They usually approach tourists and ask them the time (*que hora es?*) or their nationality.

Male prostitution has also risen considerably in Cuba. This is not regular male prostitution, but rather a means of extracting whatever they can from foreigners. A bit of innocent conversation, and you feel almost obliged to invite them out for the evening with you, pay their way into a bar and buy them a few drinks. Then comes the story of the poor family in need (a sick mother or father...), fabricated 90% of the time. Cubans have a strong sense of dignity, and true friends will rarely ask you to pay their admission fees to a nightclub, and certainly will not ask you to give them money to help their family.

Women Travellers

Women travelling alone should not encounter any problems. For the most part, people are friendly and not aggressive. Generally, men are respectful toward women, and harassment is uncommon, although Cuban males do have a tendency to flirt. Of course, a certain level of caution should be exercised; for example, avoid walking around alone in poorly lit areas at night.

Climate

There are three seasons in Cuba: the cool season (from December to April), the rainy season (from May to August) and finally the hurricane season which affects the Gulf of Mexico coast from September to November. The cool season is the most pleasant, as the heat is less stifling, the rain less frequent and the humidity lower. Daytime temperatures hover between 21 and 25°C, with cooler nights. It is still feasible, however, to travel during the rainy season, when the showers are heavy but short. Rain is most frequent from May to mid-June. In the rainy season, the average temperature is 30°C. The number of hours of daylight remains fairly constant throughout the year.

Packing

The type of clothing required does not vary much from season to season. In general, loose-fitting, comfortable cotton or linen clothes are best. When exploring urban areas, wear closed shoes that cover the entire foot rather than sandals, as they will protect against cuts that could become infected. Bring a sweater or long-sleeved shirt for cool evenings, and rubber sandals (thongs or flip-flops) to wear at the beach and in the shower. During the rainy season, an umbrella is useful for staying dry during brief tropical showers. To visit certain attractions you must wear a skirt that covers the knees or long pants. For evenings out, you might need more formal clothes, as a number of places have dress codes. Finally, if you expect to go hiking in the mountains, bring along some good hiking boots and warmer clothes.

Exchange Rates*

$1 CAN = $0.67 US	$1 US = $1.48 CAN
1 £ = $1.41 US	$1 US = 0.71 £
$1 AUS = $0.56 US	$1 US = $1.80 AUS
$1 NZ = $0.42 US	$1 US = $2.36 NZ
1 guilder = $0.39 US	$1 US = 2.55 guilders
1 EURO = $0.86 US	$1 US = 1.16 EURO
1 DM = $0.44 US	$1 US = 2.26 DM
1 SF = $0.57 US	$1 US = 1.76 SF
10 BF = $0.21 US	$1 US = 46.64 BF
100 PTA = $0.52 US	$1 US = 192.38 PTA
1000 ITL = $0.45 US	$1 US = 2,238.72 ITL
1 Peso = $0.11 US	$1 US = 9.28 Peso

* Sample only – rates fluctuate.

Practical
Information

Money and Banking

Currency

Three types of currency are legal tender in Cuba: the peso, the convertible peso and the U.S. dollar. The U.S. dollar has been legal tender since 1994 and it makes it much easier to pay for a range of goods and services. Hotels, restaurants, boutiques, as well as taxis, car rental companies, and airline and train companies only accept U.S. dollars. Finally, distinct from the Cuban peso is the convert-

ible peso, which has the same value as the U.S. dollar, but only in Cuba. Before your departure, be sure to exchange your convertible pesos for U.S. dollars, either at your hotel or at the airport.

If you spend time in Havana, you will eventually need some pesos, the *moneda nacional*. Buses, ferries, some taxis, numerous restaurants, cafés and snacks sold on street corners are all paid for with pesos. A few pesos generously given will usually open doors closed to tourists. There is now a kind of specialized bank that legally changes dollars for pesos. There is one on Calle Obispo at the corner of Calle Compostela in Old Havana. Otherwise, the best thing is to go to the *agromercados*, where there is always someone willing to change some pesos for you. Taxi drivers can also be helpful. Only change a little at a time: at 20 pesos to the dollar and considering that a coffee on the street only costs a peso, it goes a long way.

Banks and Currency Exchange

The **Banco Financiero Internacional** *(Mon to Fri 8:30am to 3pm; Linea no. 1, Vedado, ☎33-3423)* exchanges currency and can also help you with other banking transactions. It's usually crowded though, you'll have a wait. You can also go to the **Banco Nacional de Cuba-Sucursal Internacional** *(Mon to Fri 8:30am to 1pm; Calle M, at the corner of Linea, Vedado, ☎33-4241)*.

Most hotels have a **Cadeca** currency exchange office. The rates are generally the same as at local banks. These places will also cash traveller's cheques. To carry out either of these transactions, you must show your passport.

Traveller's Cheques

It is always best to keep most of your money in traveller's cheques, which are accepted in some restaurants, hotels and shops (only if they are in U.S. dollars). They are also easy to cash in banks and exchange offices as long as they were not issued by a U.S. – based bank. American Express cheques will be refused. Always keep a copy of the serial numbers of your cheques in a separate place; this way, if the cheques are lost, the company can replace them quickly and easily. Nevertheless, always carry some cash.

Credit Cards

Credit cards are accepted in some stores and restaurants, and in all hotels. Only Visa and MasterCard are accepted; American Express cards and all other cards issued by U.S. banks are systematically refused. The following cards are accepted at the Banco Financiero Internacional and in several hotels in the country, as long as they were not issued by a U.S. bank: Access, Banamex, Bancomer, Diners Club International, Eurocard,

MasterCard, Carnet, Jcb, Visa.

Mail and Telecommunications

Post Offices

The most reliable way to send mail from Havana is to use the postal services in the big hotels; the one in the Habana Libre is open 24 hours a day. A few private companies provide efficient national and international service for priority mail: **DHL Mensajeria Mundial** (*Mon to Fri 9am to 6pm, Sat 9am to noon; Avenida 1, at the corner of 42, Miramar, ☎29-3318)*, **CUBAPOST** (*Mon to Fri 8am to 4pm, Sat 8am to 2pm; Avenida 5 no. 8210, at the corner of Calle 112, ☎33-0483*) and **CUBAPACKS** (*Mon to Fri 8:30am to noon and 1:30pm to 5:30pm; Calle 22 no. 4115, Kohly, ☎24-2134*).

The **Tele Correos** company provides telephone, fax and mail services. It is located at the airport and in certain tourist areas.

Telephone and Fax

International telephone calls can be made from the larger hotels or from the few large international telecommunication centres. It is impossible to make collect calls from hotels and telecommunications centres. The only way to make a collect call is from a private residence. Pre-paid phone cards are available throughout the country for $10 and $20, but they can only be used in public phones adapted for this purpose. Before buying one of these cards, ensure that one of these phones is located nearby.

The rates for calling overseas are quite high. To avoid any unpleasant surprises, take the time to ask the rate per minute before making your call.

The staff at the telecommunications centres will explain how to make overseas calls in Spanish, or if you are lucky, in broken English.

Internet

The spider is far from having spun its web on Cuban soil. Only the State has access to the Internet and other users must find clandestine networks if they really want to get on line.

At the **Capitolio** (*at Paseo Martí and Calle Brasil*), it is possible to use the Internet for a monthly fee, but this option is strictly limited to those staying in the country for a long period of time for business purposes.

To date, travellers who wish to send and/or receive E-mail can only do so at a major hotel offering this service, for a considerable fee. Moreover, you will have to use the hotel's E-mail address and server, which means you cannot access your own E-mail account at home. Nevertheless, you can still use the hotel's E-mail to send and receive messages. Remember to bring the addresses of those to whom you wish to send sunny holiday greetings. To give you an idea of prices, this service costs $2 to send a message and $1 to receive a message at the **Hotel Nacional** (see p 148) *(at the Malecón and Calle 23, 6th floor, Oficina Ejecutiva)*.

Holidays

All banks and many businesses close on official holidays. Plan ahead by cashing traveller's cheques and doing last-minute souvenir shopping the day before. Things generally slow down during holidays.

January 1:	New Year's Day
May 6:	Labour Day
July 26:	Anniversary of the attack on the Cuartel Moncada
October 8:	Anniversary of the death of Che Guevara
October 10:	Anniversary of the beginning of the wars of independence of 1868

Miscellaneous

Tour Guides

You will likely be approached in tourist areas by Cubans speaking broken English, offering their services as tour guides. Some of them are quite capable and trustworthy, but many have little valuable information to share. Be careful. If you want to hire a guide, ask for proof of his or her qualifications. These guides not only do not work for free, but often charge a substantial fee. Before starting off on a guided tour, establish precisely what services you will be getting at what price, and pay only when the tour is over.

Alcohol

Alcohol, most often rum and beer, is sold in all little grocery stores.

Smokers

There are no restrictions with respect to smokers, Cuba being the cigar capital of the world. Some restaurants in big hotels have no-smoking sections.

Tipping

Good service is generally rewarded with a tip. In addition to the 10% service charge automatically added to the bill, a 10% to 15% tip should be left depending on the quality of the service.

Time Zones

Cuba is on Eastern Standard Time and therefore six hours behind continental Europe and five hours behind Great Britain.

Electricity

Like in North America, wall sockets take plugs with two flat pins and work on an alternating current of 110 volts (60 cycles). European visitors with electric appliances will therefore need both an adaptor and a converter.

Practical
Information

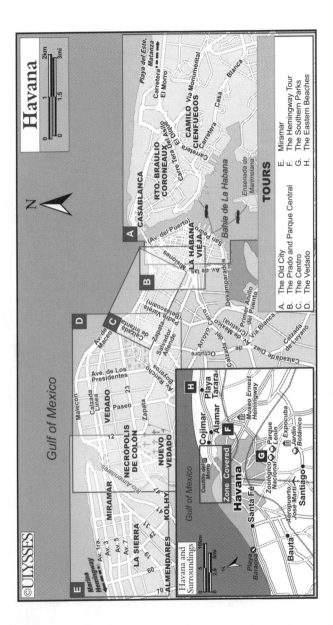

Havana

Gulf of Mexico

Playa del Este,
Matanzas

Carretera
El Morro

CAMILO
CIENFUEGOS

Casa
Blanca

Carretera

CASABLANCA

RTO. BRAULIO
CORONEAUX

Carre Tera Del
Calle Tera Del Asilo

Ensenada de
Marimelena

Bahía de La Habana

A

(Av. del Puerto)

San Pedro

LA HABANA
VIEJA

Av. de las
Misiones

B

Desamparados

Av. de las

Primer Anillo
del Puerto

Vía Blanca

Calzada
de Luyanó

Arroyo Cerro

Av. de México
(Cristina)

Zapata

Calzada del
Primer Anillo
(Belascoaín)

Padre Varela

Salvador
Allende

Calzada de Diez de
Octubre

C

Cazada
de Infanta

Av. de
Maceo

D

Ave. de Los
Presidentes

Av. Rancho
Boyeros

Malecón

Calzada
Línea

23

Paseo

VEDADO

12

NECRÓPOLIS
DE COLÓN

NUEVO
VEDADO

Río Almendares

MIRAMAR

Av. 1ra.
Marina
Hemingway

Av. 3
Av. 5
Av. 7

LA SIERRA

31
42

61

60

70

KOHLY

ALMENDARES

E

Havana and Surroundings

Gulf of Mexico

Playa
Baracoa

Castillo del Morro

Zone Covered

Havana

Santa Fé

Bauta

Aeropuerto
José Martí

Santiago

Cojímar

Alamar

Playa
Tarará

H

Museo Ernest
Hemingway

F

Zoológico
Nacional

Parque
Lenin

Expocuba
Jardín
Botánico

G

TOURS

A. The Old City
B. The Prado and Parque Central
C. The Centro
D. The Vedado

E. Miramar
F. The Hemingway Tour
G. The Southern Parks
H. The Eastern Beaches

© ULYSSES

Exploring

Havana has many tourist attractions. From Habana Vieja to Miramar, the town unfolds in splendour in a multitude of magnificent images.

The narrow streets and colonial buildings of the old city, Parque Central and the surrounding neoclassical architecture, the lively Centro and the grand homes of the Vedado and Miramar all evoke the incredibly rich history of the place.

Havana is one of the most beautiful cities in the world, and it is worth doing a little digging around in its past. Its history has marked it with an east-west orientation, which is probably the best axis around which to appreciate it.

Tour A:
The Old City

Declared a World Heritage Site by UNESCO in 1982, Habana Vieja (Old Havana) is truly the touristic centre of the city. Its restoration is well underway, which may make you feel as if you were walking in the middle of a huge construction site. The tourists here are legion, which is not surprising considering the impressive number of colonial buildings that are crammed into this part of the capital. Some of them are veritable jewels of the colonial baroque style.

The focus on tourism to boost the country's foreign currency is starting to bear fruit. Habaguanex, which is charged with commercializing the old town, projected direct benefits of more than $50 million for the year 2000, and most of this money will be reinvested in the current restoration project. This work is being carried out under the watchful eye of the Historiador de la Ciudad, who sees that everything possible is done to preserve the historical and architectural character of the area.

Habana Vieja consists of two areas that are distinct both in terms of their history and their architecture: the old city, the section that was historically surrounded by a high wall and whose architecture is decidedly baroque, and the Prado and Parque Central Sector which extends to the west beyond the boundaries mentioned

previously. For the sake of clarity, this tour only looks at the first of these two zones, the old city, that is, Habana Vieja within the walls. Bordered on the east by the port and its mouth, and on the west by Avenida de las Misiones, Avenida de Bélgica and Avenida Egido, this section forms the heart of the colonial town. Tour B looks at the Prado and Parque Central.

The touristic development of the old city started with its large squares, or *plazas*, and is extending out from them to the neighbouring streets. Between the Plaza de Armas, Plaza de la Catedral, Plaza de San Francisco and the Plaza Vieja, the major points of interest are located in a relatively restricted area. Thus it is possible to cover the essence of the old city in a short time by walking along Mercaderes and Obispo streets. It can also be interesting to let yourself roam beyond this tour to take in the place and really get a feeling for the atmosphere. A detour southwards will add tremendously to the experience of your visit.

Since tourism is flourishing in this part of the town, it is worth going there early in the morning to really get the most out of it. Otherwise, you might find your-

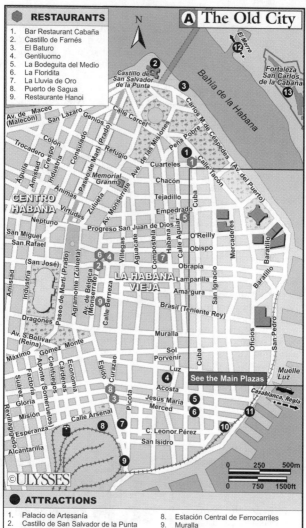

RESTAURANTS

1. Bar Restaurant Cabaña
2. Castillo de Farnés
3. El Baturo
4. Gentiluomo
5. La Bodeguita del Medio
6. La Floridita
7. La Lluvia de Oro
8. Puerto de Sagua
9. Restaurante Hanoi

A The Old City

N

El Morro

Castillo de San Salvador de la Punta

Fortaleza San Carlos de la Cabaña

Bahía de la Habana

Av. de Maceo (Malecón)

San Lázaro
Genios
Calle Cárcel
Carlos M de Céspedes (Av. del Puerto)
Peña Pobre

Trocadero
Colón
Consulado
Refugio
Paseo de Martí (Prado)
Ave. de las Misiones
Cuarteles
Cuba
Calle Tacón

Crespo
Industria
Aguila
Amistad
Animas
Memorial Granma
Chacón
Tejadillo
Empedrado

CENTRO HABANA
Neptuno
Virtudes
Zulueta
Av. Monserrate
Progreso San Juan de Dios
O'Reilly
Mercaderes
Baratillo

San Miguel
San Rafael
Villegas
Aguacate
Compostela
Habana
Calle Aguiar
Obispo

(San José)
Agramonte (Zulueta)
Av. de Bélgica (Monserrate)
Calle Berneza
LA HABANA VIEJA
Obrapía
Lamparilla
Amargura
San Ignacio
Obispo

Amistad
Industria
Paseo de Martí (Prado)
Dragones
Brasil (Teniente Rey)

Av. S. Bolívar (Reina)
Máximo Gómez Monte
Muralla
Muralla
Oficios
San Pedro

Cienfuegos
Aponte (Someruelos)
Cárdenas
Economia
Egido
Calle Curazao
Picota
Sol
Porvenir
Luz

Suárez
Factoría
Gloria
Misión
Esperanza
Alcantarilla
Revillagigedo
Calle Arsenal
Acosta
Jesús María
Merced
C. Leonor Pérez
San Isidro
Muelle Luz
Casablanca, Regla
See the Main Plazas

©ULYSSES

0   250   500m
0   750   1500ft

ATTRACTIONS

1. Palacio de Artesanía
2. Castillo de San Salvador de la Punta
3. Statue de Pierre Le Moyne d'Iberville
4. Conviento de Belén
5. Iglesia Espiritu Santo
6. Iglesia de la Merced
7. Casa Natal José Martí
8. Estación Central de Ferrocarriles
9. Muralla
10. Iglesia de San Francisco de Paula
11. Almenada de Paula
12. Castillo de los Tres Reyes del Morro
13. Fortaleza San Carlos de la Cabaña

self overwhelmed by hoards of tourists and their guides.

The Main Plazas

It is easy to make your way from one of the four main *plazas* to another without getting too tired and thus get a taste, in a short time, of Havana's most beautiful, but also most touristic, offerings. Each of these squares is separated from its neighbours by short distances that you can easily cover via one of the magnificent little streets lined with charming colonial houses. Many of these have been renovated and turned into restaurants, hotels or museums. All along the way there are numerous terraces to gratify all tastes. Emerging from them you can hear the strains of musicians playing Cuban music, which lends the whole area a delightful atmosphere.

Several small museums have been established in former homes and palaces that were built near the *plazas*, the commercial and political centres of the city. At the town museum on the Plaza de Armas, you can purchase a $9 pass that lets you into

a dozen of these museums, which is not bad considering that some places are now charging entrance fees of up to $3.

★★★
Plaza de la Catedral

Plaza de la Catedral is a good place to start off a tour of the old city. It was the last square laid out inside the city walls and it is a charming spot where the architecture of the old town is revealed in all its splendour. The **Catedral de La Havana** ★★★ (*Calle Empedrado no.158*), has one of the most beautiful baroque facades in all of Latin America. Begun in 1748, the church was not completed and consecrated as a cathedral until 1789, when Havana was elevated to the rank of a bishopric. Flanked by two asymmetrical towers, it completely dominates

Catedral de La Habana

the large square. The interior, redone over the course of the 19th century, might disappoint lovers of the baroque, but the whole place does nevertheless have a certain charm.

Opposite the cathedral, on the other side of the *plaza*, is a colonial house that now serves as the **Museo de Arte Colonial** ★ *($2; every day, 9am to 7pm; Calle San Ignacio no.61, ☎62-6440)*. Built in 1720 for the governor of Cuba, Luis Chacón, the building is characteristic of houses of that era, with a central courtyard surrounded by galleries, arches and roofs made of carved wood. Founded in 1969, the museum contains a small collection of colonial-style furniture and decorative objects and a room devoted to the means of transportation of this period.

Between the two, to the right of the cathedral, the former **Palacio de los Marqueses de Aguas Claras**, built in 1760, is now home to the El Patio restaurant, whose terrace is probably the most coveted in Habana Vieja. It is worth going in and taking a look at the restaurant's interior patio, one of the most beautiful in the city.

The many craftspeople, who a little while ago crammed the square, have

Patio of the Palacio de Artesanía

now been relegated to the Calle Tacón, to the east, in front of the magnificent **Seminario San Carlos.** Completed in 1774, it is still used as a seminary and is unfortunately not open to visitors, but the exterior alone is worth a detour.

Just in front of the seminary is the **Parque Luz Caballero**, a lovely park where you can breathe a little bay air and watch the boats go through the narrows out to sea or into port. From there, there is a lovely view of the Morro and La Cabaña forts. You can go a little farther north to see the **Palacio de Artesanía** ★ *(Calle Cuba no. 64, between Calle Cuarteles and Calle Pena Pobre)*.

Exploring

Formerly the palace of Count Pedroso, one of the richest and most influential men in the colony, the residence was built in 1780. It was occupied in the second half of the 19th century by the city's court house. Its interior courtyard is an utter delight, and its double veranda, the only one of its kind in Havana, is especially pleasant. The Palacio de Artesanía is currently occupied by craft shops and a restaurant/bar.

Two of the most important 20th-century Cuban artists are now well established on the street near the Plaza de la Catedral. A magnificent colonial house dating from 1760 and formerly known as the Casa de los Condes de San Fernando de Peñalver, the **Centro Wilfredo Lam** ★★ *($2; Calle San Ignacio, at the corner of Calle Empedrado)* displays works by contemporary artists from Cuba and various Latin American countries. but unfortunately nothing by Wilfredo Lam (1902-1982), the internationally renowned Cuban painter

● ATTRACTIONS

1. Plaza de la Catedral
2. Catedral de la Habana
3. Museo de Arte Colonial
4. Seminario San Carlos
5. Parque Luz Caballero
6. Centro Wilfredo Lam
7. Museo Alejo Carpentier
8. Gabinete Arqueologico
9. Plaza de Armas
10. Castillo de la Real Fuerza
11. Templete
12. Museo de la Ciudad
13. Palacio del Secundo Cabo
14. Museo de Historia Natural
15. Mirador de la Bahía
16. Museo de la Plata
17. Museo de Autos Antiguos
18. Casa del Arabe
19. Museo Numismático
20. Casa del Benemérito de las Américas Benito Juárez
21. Museo Taller Guayasamín
22. Casa de África
23. Casa de la Obrapía
24. Maqueta del Centro Histórico
25. Plaza de San Francisco
26. Fuente de los Leones
27. Basílica de San Francisco
28. Plaza Vieja
29. Casa de los Condes de Jaruco
30. Iglesia San Francisco
31. Museo Nacional de la Historia de las Sciencias Carlos J.Finlay
32. Conviento de Santa Clara
33. Fundación Havana Club
34. Museo Alexander de Humboldt

◯ ACCOMMODATIONS

1. Ambos Mundos
2. Hotel Conde de Villanueva
3. Hotel Florida
4. Hotel del Tejadillo
5. Hostal El Comendador
6. Hostal Valencia
7. Residencia Académica del Convento de Santa Clara
8. Santa Isabel

● RESTAURANTS

1. Café de Oriente
2. Café Paris
3. Cafetería Torre La Vega
4. D' Giovanni's
5. El Patio
6. La Dominica
7. La Mina
8. Los Dos Hermanos
9. Los Marinos
10. Restaurante Al Medina
11. Torre de Marfil

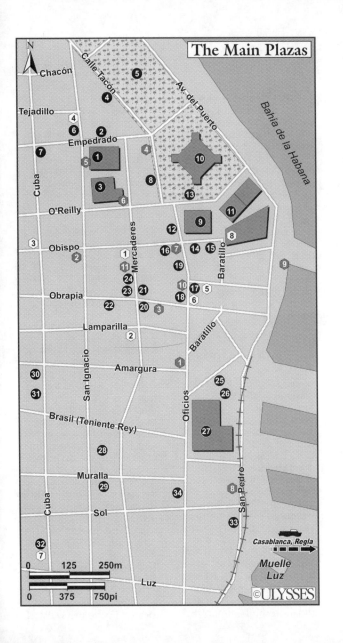

The Main Plazas

N

Chacón

Calle Tacón

Av. del Puerto

Bahía de la Habana

Tejadillo

Empedrado

Cuba

O'Reilly

Obispo

Mercaderes

Baratillo

Obrapía

Lamparilla

Baratillo

Amargura

San Ignacio

Oficios

Brasil (Teniente Rey)

Muralla

Cuba

Sol

San Pedro

Luz

Casablanca, Regla

Muelle Luz

0   125   250m

0   375   750pi

©ULYSSES

whose name the centre bears.

Literature buffs should make sure to visit the house that helped inspire Cuban author Alejo Carpentier to write one of his major works, *Siglo de los Luces*. The **Museo Alejo Carpentier** *(free admission; 8:30am to 3:30pm; Calle Empedrado no. 215)* is very peaceful and sure to catch your fancy. Numerous original manuscripts by the author are on display, and there is a guide to accompany you on your tour. The museum also has a research centre and a library, where many Carpentier experts come to work.

★★★
Plaza de Armas

To get from the Plaza de la Catedral to the Plaza de Armas, which is only a few steps away, you can take the Calle Mercaderes, or you can go right along the Calle Tacón, a charming street that goes the length of the Castillo de la Real Fuerza, and stop on the way at the little **Gabinete Arcqueologico ★** *(entrance free; Tue to Sat 9am to 5pm, Sun 9am to 1pm; 12 Calle Tacón, between Calle O'Reilly and Calle Empredado)*, situated in a 17th-century residence. You can still see some of the murals that added to the beauty of the place. The ceilings on the second floor are in the *mudéjar* style (a moorish style originating in Spain) that was characteristic of this era. The Gabinete Arqueologico exhibits objects that date back to the early days of the colony, and there is a room containing some interesting objects associated with indigenous culture.

The Plaza de Armas is the oldest square in Havana. The first mass on the site of the new colony was celebrated here in 1519. It is a magnificent square graced with a park of flowering trees where you can shelter from the midday sun surrounded by tables of second-hand books for sale. The political centre of the colony for almost the entire period of Spanish domination, it is surrounded by the most beautiful baroque buildings in the old city. In the centre of this square, which is such a powerful reminder of the Spanish takeover of this city and the whole country, it is interesting to find a statue of **Carlos Manuel de Cespedes**, the very man who launched the first war of independence in 1868 with his *Grito de Yara*.

The square was originally used for military exercises by soldiers stationed in this New World outpost. It is located inside the walls of the oldest fortress of the city, **Castillo de la Real Fuerza**. Built in 1577 to defend against the threat of pirates, it now houses the **Museo Nacional de la Real Fuerza** ★★ (*$1; every day 9am to 5pm; Calle O'Reilly, between Avenida del Puerto and Calle Tacón*). The museum contains a large collection of ceramics, including lovely pieces by renowned Cuban sculptors Wilfredo Lam (1902-1982) and René Porto Carrero (1912-1985). Two galleries are used for exhibitions of contemporary art. The castle is very well preserved. The pleasant rooftop terrace offers a unique view of the Christ of Havana, on the other side of the bay, and of Habana Vieja in general. On the northwest tower of the castle, you'll see **La Giraldilla**, the symbol of the city .

The **Templete** (*$1; every day 9am to 5pm; corner of Baratillo and O'Reilly*) is the first neoclassical building in Havana. It memorializes the official founding of the city in 1519 by Panfilio de Narváez, who was acting on the orders of Spanish conquistador Diego Velázquez. Each year on November 16, each year, the first mass ever to have been celebrated in Havana is commemorated here. This historic moment is depicted inside in a fresco by French artist Jean-Baptiste Vermany.

The **Museo de la Ciudad** ★★★ (*$3; Tue to Sat 9am to 5pm, Sun 9am to 1pm; Calle Tacón, between Calle Obispo and Calle O'Reilly, ☎61-2876*), also on the Plaza de Armas, is devoted to the city of Havana and is a must for all visitors to the Cuban capital. The building is the former Palacio de los Capitanes Generales. It was here that the Treaty of Paris, which placed Cuba under U.S. control, was signed in 1898. During the U.S. occupation (1898-1902), and until 1920, the palace was the seat of the Cuban presidency. It then served as the city hall until 1958. The palace's baroque architecture makes it one of the finest in Havana. Reigning over the inner courtyard is a statue of Christopher Columbus in Italian marble, which dates from 1862. It stands in the shadow of two royal palms, the official emblem of Cuba. A historical and architectural treasure, this museum contains numerous works of art and colonial objects, all attractively displayed.

Right next to the city museum is the **Palacio del Segundo Cabo** ★★, which was built in 1772. It vies with the Palacio de los Capitanes Generales, built

Exploring

La Giraldilla

La Giraldilla, the first bronze-cast statue in Havana, is a tribute to Inés de Bobadilla, the wife of Hernando de Soto, Governor of Cuba, and the victim of a lost dream.

Hernando de Soto, who was with Pizarro during the conquest of Peru, believed that Florida concealed riches surpassing those that the conquistadors had found in the new lands belonging to the Spanish crown. He invested the 100,000 ducats he had brought back from Peru in an expedition to North America. Confident of success, he brought his wife and all his belongings with him. As Governor of Cuba, he could use the island as a jumping off point for his expeditions to Florida, which at this time consisted of the entire southern part of the United States.

At the end of May 1539, de Soto left for Florida with nine ships, 237 horses, 513 men and enough provisions for a whole year. Preparations for the expedition completely drained the island of Cuba of its resources. The conquistador left his wife with the responsibility of governing while he was away helping himself to the riches he believed were at his fingertips.

De Soto did not find what he was looking for. The Florida empire eluded him and he perished on the banks of the Mississippi. His body was abandoned by the few survivors who eventually made their way to the Spanish colony of Panuco some three years after the expedition had landed on the peninsula.

The news of her husband's death only reached Inés de Bobadilla in October 1543. Until then, the faithful wife had refused to believe her husband was dead; for three years, she had watched for a sign of his return from high in the tower of Castillo de la Real Fuerza.

The little statue has become a symbol for the city. The one at the Castillo is a copy, the original being in the city museum.

in the same period, as the old city's most beautiful example of baroque *herreriano* architecture. Under the Spanish it served as the commissionership, the bureau of internal affairs and then the post office. In the first years of the Republic it was the Senate, and when the latter moved to Capitolio, it became the Supreme Court. It is now the home of the Cuban Institute of Books and a large, well-stocked bookstore. In return for a small tip, you can ask to go onto the roof of the building which offers an entrancing view of the fort.

In front of the Palacio del Secundo Cabo, on the other side of the square, you will find the natural history museum **Museo de Historia Natural** *($3; every day 9:30am to 6:30pm; Calle Obispo no. 61, between Calle Mercaderes and Calle Officios)* in the building that was the U.S. embassy under the Republic. The modernity of the interior

contrasts starkly with the surrounding buildings, and the exhibitions do not hold much interest. There is a large section on the fauna and flora of Cuba on the second floor.

The **Mirador de la Bahía** ★ is located on the roof of a building next to the natural history museum, on Calle Obispo. The view of the bay from here is sublime, and there is a cafeteria that serves light meals and drinks. The restaurant is rather ordinary, but it is a pleasant place to have a drink. To get to the Mirador, take the entrance to the left of the entrance to the natural history museum and go right to the end of the corridor to the elevator, which will take you up there in seconds.

Still on Calle Obispo, just behind the city museum, is the **Museo de la Plata** *($1; Tue to Sat 9am to 5pm, Sun 9am to 1pm; Calle Obispo, between Calle Officios and Calle*

Exploring

Mercaderes). A sort of annex to the city museum, it exhibits an impressive collection of silverware.

★
Plaza de Armas to Plaza de San Francisco

Between the Plaza de Armas and the Plaza de San Francisco, there are several period houses that have been refurbished and turned into museums or cultural centres.

The **Museo de Autos Antiguos** *($1; Mon to Sun 9am to 6:30pm; Calle Oficios, between Calle Obispo and Calle Obrapía)* displays a collection of vintage cars of considerable historical interest, including the first car to have arrived in Havana (a 1905 Cadillac) and Che Guevara's Chevrolet.

The **Casa del Arabe** *($1; Tue to Sat 9am to 5pm; Calle Officios no.12, between Calle Obispo and Calle Obrapía)*, built in 1688 and perfectly maintained in its original state, presents ethnological and cultural exhibitions on Arab and Muslim societies.

The nearby **Museo Numismático** *($1; Tue to Sat 10am to 5pm; Sun 9am to 1pm; Calle Oficios no. 8, between Calle Obispo and Calle Obrapía, ☎61-5857)* has

a large collection of Cuban coins.

Dedicated to Mexican culture and history, the **Casa del Benemérito de Las Américas Benito Juarez** *(free admission; Tue to Sun 9:30am to 5pm; Calle Obrapía no. 116, at the corner of Calle Mercaderes, ☎61-8166)* presents exhibitions on the popular crafts of Mexico.

The **Museo-Taller Guayasamín** ★ *($1; Tue to Sat 10:30am to 5pm; Sun 9am to 1pm; Calle Obrapía no. 111, between Mercaderes and Oficios, ☎61-3843)*, across the street, is the Havana studio of celebrated Ecuadorian painter and sculptor Guayasamín, who died in 1999. You can visit his bedroom and studio, and see a few of his canvases, including a huge portrait of the Commandante, who was a personal friend of the artist.

Right nearby, the **Casa de Africa** *($2; Tue to Sat 10:30am to 12:30pm and 2pm to 4pm, Sun 10am to noon; Calle Obrapía no. 15, between Mercaderes and San Ignacio, ☎61-5798)* houses two large collections of objects related to the various Afro-Cuban religions. A number of its galleries are devoted exclusively to African culture. While you're in the neighbourhood, you can also stop by the historic **Casa de la Obrapía** *(free admis-*

sion; Tue to Sat 10:30am to 4pm, Sun 9am to 1pm; Calle Obrapía no. 158, at the corner of Mercaderes, ☎61-3097), the former residence of Spanish captain Martín Calvo de la Puerta. Dating back to 1648, this house was enlarged and remodelled in the 18th century and still has some of its original murals. Also on display is some furniture from the 19th century, and one of the rooms on the main floor is devoted to the memory of the Cuban writer Alejo Carpentier.

To get a better sense of the old city, you can look at the magnificent **Maqueta del Centro Histórico ★** *($1; every day 9am to 6:30pm; Mercaderes 116, between Calle Obispo and Calle Obrapia)*. On a larger scale than the one in the Miramar, this model gives a clear and intelligible sense of the space in the historic centre of Havana. Those who want to get the most out of their Havana experience will find the guides' explanations very useful.

★★
Plaza de San Francisco

The Plaza de San Francisco is the second-oldest square in the city. Its proximity to the port made it an important commercial centre right from the beginning of the

colony. Since the 1980s, work has been going on to restore its former lustre. The large square is surrounded by magnificent buildings and residences, and the grandeur of the square is enhanced by the **Fuente de los Leones**, built in 1836. The terraces adjoining the square constantly reverberate with Cuban music, which gives the place a wonderful atmosphere.

But it is the **Basílica de San Francisco ★★** *($2; every day 9am to 6:30pm; entrance on Calle Officios, between Calle Amargura and Calle Brasil)* that really gives the square its grandeur. Facing the interior of the town, the front of the basilica is perhaps difficult to appreciate fully, but it is worth the effort. Completed in 1739 with the convent that extended it, this church gives an unparalleled picture of the austerity of this architectural movement, the simple and severe baroque style of which there are very few examples in the world. In the evenings it is turned into a concert hall. The convent houses a museum of religious and secular art that should not be missed.

★★
Plaza Vieja

It is a short walk on Calle Brasil from the Plaza de San

Exploring

Solares

Solares are large houses that have been transformed into several flats and are shared by numerous families. Old Havana is full of them. This is how Guillermo Cabrera Infante (our translation) places them in the city's history:

"I have already explained, briefly, how I imagine that these buildings, divided up into rooms (not like the co-operatives on Zulueta Street, but the authentic ones, the very first stately homes in Old Havana), got the name solar. *These old houses, abandoned by their noble or ennobled owners after Independence, were divided into rooms in order to absorb, not only the expanding population of Havana, but also people moving from* the countryside in the first years of the Republic. And the guérilleros mambís, not the officers but the army rabble composed mainly of poor whites, blacks and mulattos, moved into these houses as well. The white officers invaded the grand Havana homes outside the walls on the continuation of Zulueta and Monserrat streets; here they would become the new aristocrats and create caricature colonies at Cerro, Vibora and as far away as Vedado. This is the way the noble houses of the old city, the* solariegas *houses, became* solares."

Taken from *La Habana para un infante difiunto*, published in 1979.

Francisco to the recently restored Plaza Vieja. From the 16th century, the Plaza Vieja was an outdoor market, and for some time it was the largest slave market in the city. While they were at it, some rich merchants established themselves on the square in order to be close to their businesses. City authorities are currently turning this square into a beauty, the latest to take advantage of the serious renovation effort underway. With a pretty fountain at its centre and the old houses surrounding it, some still arranged as *solares*, it will be charming.

There are many residences and palaces around the square, but only the **Casa de los Condes de Jaruco** ★ (*107 Calle Muralla, corner of Calle San Ignacio*) is open to the public. This old residence was built in the 1730s and now houses a cultural centre and a variety of craft shops.

From the Vieja Plaza, you can take Calle San Ignacio up towards Plaza de la Catedral, or by taking Calle Mercaderes, return to Plaza de Armas.

Walk to the Two Forts

Between the Castillo de la Real Fuerza on the Plaza de Armas and the Castillo de San Salvador de la Punta, at the entrance to the bay, there is a pleasant walk where you can see how narrow the mouth of the bay really is by watching the enormous liners, which glide through very carefully. The view from here of the forts built on the promontory on the other side of the waterway is magnificent. The air here is always a bit cooler than in the maze of narrow streets in the old city, and there is something

relaxing about the sight of the fishers casting their lines surrounded by small boats drifting on the waves. Well kept and pleasant, in spite of the cars constantly passing on the busy Avenida Carlos Manuel de Cespedes, it is one of the loveliest places to breathe in the sea air and the atmosphere of Havana.

Just before you arrive at the **Castillo de San Salvador de la Punta**, a fortress (currently under renovation) that was built at the end of the 16th century to secure the entrance to the bay, you will see the statue of **Pierre Le Moyne d'Iberville**. This statue of a Canadian who died within the town walls in 1706 is an indication of just how deeply the memory of this brilliant navigator has become rooted in Havana.

Tour of the South

Those who would like to extend their experience in Habana Vieja, but want to escape the touristic jungle around the main plazas, should head south. Not only are there a number of important sites in the streets of this part of the city, but you will also see a more authentic aspect of Cuban life.

Exploring

From Iberville to Havana

Pierre Le Moyne d'Iberville was born in the heart of New France, at Ville Marie (Montreal), in 1662. After having made life difficult for the British in the northern part of North America, and started the Louisiana colony for France at the mouth of the Mississippi, at the beginning of the 18th century, he made great plans to secure the future of the French Empire in America.

Havana's strategic importance was central to his concern. It appeared evident to him that whoever controlled Havana controlled the Gulf of Mexico and thus the southern entry to the North American continent. If the mouth of the Mississippi were to fall into the hands of the British, it would be easy for them to take the French Empire from behind. What worried Iberville was that the Spanish did not seem to realize the danger that threatened them. They had only one fort in Florida, Fort San Agustín, which was in a pitiful state. Iberville was sure that at the first opportunity, the British would take over the fort and then cross the strait from Florida to take possession of the island of Cuba and its main port. According to Iberville's strategy, there was only one way to keep this from happening: the British colonies had to be attacked and destabilized before they could mount an offensive.

From 1702 to 1705, Iberville fiercely defended his plan before the king and his ministers in Versailles, and on August 20, 1705, he was given carte blanche to mount an expedition that would take him first to the British West Indies. He had orders to cause maximum damage and confusion there before advancing to the Carolinas and then farther north up the coast to Newfoundland, taking care not to leave any enemy ships afloat.

It was a grandiose plan, but Iberville believed he could carry it out.

Only in the spring of 1706 did Iberville finally arrive in the British West Indies. As a result of untimely manoeuvres by his lieutenant, he lost the surprise advantage, which would have allowed him to attack Jamaica, the centre of British power in the Caribbean. He therefore decided to make do with the island of Nevis, which fell into his hands during the first days of April. Nevertheless, the commander of the fleet was worried about the future of his mission. The support given by the French buccaneers, hastily gathered together, did not seem adequate to fulfil his task, so asked Spain for help. With this intention in mind, Iberville arrived in Havana from Nevis by way of Saint Dominique.

What was Iberville's plan? He knew that the Spanish government had four warships that patrolled the waters between Havana and Veracruz, Mexico, and that these ships called in at the large bay each year during the month of August. He went to Cuba then, to ask the authorities to put these ships at his disposal. Unfortunately, he died mysteriously before any accord could be made. Iberville was buried July 9, 1706 in the crypt of the Church of Saint Christopher rather than in the cathedral, as numerous pious pilgrims would like to believe. No one really knows what happened to Iberville's remains after the church was destroyed in 1741.

During the first few years of the colony, the missionary and religious aspect of the venture was taken seriously, even though according to those who made a stop here Havana was not exactly a model of piety. Whether or not this is true, after the fortifications were constructed, it was the convents and churches that make the strongest impression on the urban landscape of Havana. Constructed of durable materials and with particular care, they are among the most significant architectural testimonials in the city. One could say that if the political and commercial power of the city is concentrated in and around the Plaza de Armas, it is in the southern part of the walled city that religious power is concentrated, a power that should not be taken lightly.

For an excursion into this less-known part of the colonial city, it is best to take Calle Cuba, the axis around which you will find the main attractions. This way, you will begin your tour with the **Iglesia San Francisco** (*Calle Cuba, corner of Calle Amargura*). Built in the 17th century, it is one of the oldest churches in Havana. It has retained its exterior, which was very typical of this period. Unfortunately, the same cannot be said of the interior, which was redone in the mid-19th century.

Just next door, the **Museo Nacional de la Historia de las Sciencias Carlos J. Finlay** (*$2; Mon to Fri 8:30am to 5pm, Sat 9am to 4pm; Calle Cuba no. 460, between Calle Amargura and Calle Brasil*) is located in another magnificent 17th-century building that was formerly an Augustine convent. It bears the name of the Cuban doctor who discovered that yellow fever, which was endemic all over the island, is transmitted by

a mosquito. This discovery finally enabled the Cubans to tackle this plague head on. The museum's main vocation is to make known Cuba's various scientific breakthroughs in the 19th century through documents and scientific equipment.

The magnificent **Convento de Santa Clara** ★★ (*$2; Mon to Fri 9am to 4pm; Calle Cuba, between Calle Sol and Calle Luz*) is definitely worth a visit. Built between 1638 and 1643 to house the rich young girls of the town, its patio, the largest on the island, is absolutely stunning. The convent was tremendously rich and by the end of the 18th century could count on income from 20 sugar *haciendas* to cover its day-to-day expenses. The Centro Nacional de Restauración occupies some space in two wings of the convent, but the majority of the building is open to the public. There is a small restaurant where you can quench your thirst or have a snack.

There is another convent just behind this one that is currently being completely restored: the **Convento de Belen** ★ and its church, which occupy the whole of the block bordered by the streets Compostela, Acosta, Picota and Luz. Built between 1712 and 1718 for the congregation of

Arco de Belén

Bethlehem, it is one of the most important examples of baroque architecture in the old city. Although you can't go in, the front alone is worth the trip, especially the church at the corner of Calle Luz and Calle Compostella. You should also have a look at the huge arch, the **Arco de Belén**, built in 1772 to connect the convent with the buildings on the other side of the Calle Acosta, on the Calle Compostella. This structure, supported by immense wooden beams, is unique in Havana. And to add to the charm of the place, a

most picturesque market is held in front of the convent every day.

On returning to Calle Cuba, you can ogle the magnificent **Iglesia Espiritu Santo ★★★** *(Calle Cuba, between Calle Acosta and Calle Jesús María)*. The oldest church in Havana, it was built in 1638 and has retained all the typical features of the period. Its severe facade, its immense side doors and its delicious wooden ceiling are all perfectly charming. You can also go down under the alter to see the catacombs. Until 1805, when the first cemetery was established in the city, the Spanish were buried under the alters of churches. Traces of these underground tombs have been preserved in nearly all the old churches in the city.

One street-corner lower, the **Iglesia de la Merced** (*Calle Cuba, between Calle Jesús María and Calle Merced*) bears the traces of numerous modifications. Begun in 1755, its construction was continually interrupted for various lengths of time and it was only completed in 1904. The decor contrasts sharply with the austere exterior of the church, but it is worth a look. The immense marble altarpiece is really striking.

From Calle Leonor Perez, better known as "Paula," head west to the **Casa Natal José Martí** ★ (*$1; Tue to Sat 9am to 5pm, Sun 9am to 1pm; Calle Leonor Pérez no. 314,*

between Avenda Egido and Calle Picota). This is the little house where the national hero José Martí was born in 1853. The museum tells the story of his exile in a particularly interesting way and displays a number of objects that belonged to him.

Almost in front of the house of this minstrel of Cuban independence, at the end of Avenida Egido, you will see the grandiose facade of the **Estación Central de Ferrocarriles**, built in 1912. Inside is displayed a superb train, *La Junta*, the first locomotive of the Compañia del Ferrocaril de Matanzas. This was the locomotive that inaugurated the Havana – Matanzas line in 1843.

For those who are interested, the two most beautiful sections of the old wall that surrounded the city until 1863 are in front of the railway station. The **Muralla** ★, which used to run the length of the port and continued west to follow what are now Avenida Egido, Avenida de Bélgica and Avenida Monserrate, tightly enclosed the city as a world apart. At night, with a little ceremony that is reminiscent of the cannon

Casa Natal José Martí

The Catedral de la Habana no doubt features the most beautiful baroque facade in all of Latin America.
- *P. Escudero*

Like the sea, music is omnipresent in Havana.
- *P. Escudero*

Parked in front of the Capitolio, this car is one of the many old American models on the streets of Havana. - *P. Escudero*

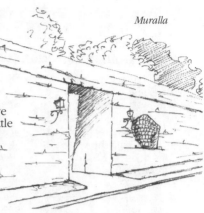

Muralla

ceremony held at 9pm every evening at the Cabaña fortress, the wall gates were closed, effectively cutting off the city of Havana from its surroundings. Some other remains of the wall have survived, such as the little section that ends at Calle Brasil, but you have to go to the end of Avenida Egido to really appreciate the size of the undertaking. When you see these sections of the wall, you really get a feeling for what this city must have been like in the 17th and 18th centuries. The last big piece of the Muralla is marked by a large bronze plaque that traces the boundaries of the old city.

When you head back up north on San Pedro, along the water, you cross the magnificent little **Iglesia de San Francisco de Paula** ★ (*at the corner of Calle Leonor Pérez and Avenida San Pedro*). Now being restored, it was built between 1730 and 1745 and was attached to a hospital of the same name. This hospital, which provided medical care to needy women, has now disappeared, but its church survived. In the 18th century it was the most beautiful church in Havana, and its nave is a real marvel. You can go in and take a peek at the interior and at the same time watch the craftspeople working on its restoration.

From Iglesia de Paula to Calle Acosta, heading up toward the Plaza de San Francisco, you will come to **Almenada de Paula**, which stretches the length of Avenida San Pedro. Built in the second half of the 18th century, it was the first promenade in the walled city and remained, until the construction of Paseo del Prado, the most fashionable one in Havana. Although there aren't many large trees to provide much-needed shade, it is still pleasant to stroll along and watch the harbour life mingling there.

Before you arrive back at the Basílica de San Francisco, there are two other interesting stops you can

Exploring

Alexander von Humboldt and Havana

The famous traveller Alexander von Humboldt knew Havana well and left a striking – although unflattering – portrait of it. This is what he writes in his book *The Island of Cuba*, published in 1826:

"The principal edifices of Havana, the Cathedral, the Government House, the residence of the Comandante of Marine, the Navy-yard, the Post-office, and the Royal Tobacco factory, are less notable for their beauty than for the solidity of their construction. The streets are generally narrow, and many of them are not paved. [...] During my residence in Spanish America [the author is writing here about his second stay, the spring of 1804] *few of the cities presented a more disgusting appearance than did Havana, from want of a good police. One walked through mud up to the knees, and many carriages, or volantes, which are the characteristic carriages of this city, and the drays laden with boxes of sugar, their drivers rudely elbowing the passer-by, made walking in the streets both vexatious and humiliating. The offensive odor of the salted meat, or tasajo, infected many of the houses, and even some of the ill-ventilated streets."*

"The city of Havana proper is surrounded by walls, and is about 1,900 yards [1,710m] long by 1060 yards [954m] wide; and yet there are piled in this narrow space 44,000 people, of which 25,000 are blacks and mulattos."

Those that have the means leave the city for better places:

"From the Punta to San Lazaro, from the Cabaña to Regla, and thence to Atarès, the land is filled with habitations; those which surround the bay being of light and elegant construction. The plan of the house is drawn, and they are ordered from the

> *United States, as one would order any piece of furniture. When the yellow fever prevails at Havana, the inhabitants retire to these country houses, and to the hills between Regla and Guanavacoa, where they breathe a purer air."*
>
> This being said, von Humboldt has a few good
>
> things to say about the city's two beautiful promenades, the Alamada (La Almenada de Paula) between Paula Hospice and the theatre, and the *"passeo extra muros"* (Prado), between Castillo de la Punta and Puerta de la Muralla, which is *"delightfully refreshing."*

make. The recently opened **Fundación Havana Club** (*every day, 9am to 6pm; Calle San Pedro no. 262, between Calle Sol and Calle Luz*), is a rum museum of sorts. Located in a magnificent house dating back to the second half of the 19th century, the museum traces all the stages of the manufacture of rum from sugar cane – the best in the world, so one learns, because of the island's soil quality. Entrance is free of charge (but this may change soon) and you get a sample with the visit.

Finally, when you leave Avenida San Pedro to return to Calle Officios, you can visit the **Museo Alexander De Humboldt** (*free admission; Tue to Sat 9am to 5pm, Sun 9am to noon; Calle Officios, between Calle Sol and Calle Muralla*).

Considered the second man to "discover" Cuba, Baron von Humboldt established his laboratory in this old house during his two visits to the island, in 1800 and 1804. You can still see some of his designs and instruments and follow his route on maps of the island hanging on the walls.

El Morro and the Cabaña

On the other side of the mouth of the the bay and port, the landscape is dominated by two of the most imposing military structures in Havana. It is difficult not to be awed by the size of these buildings.

Exploring

Castillo de los Tres Reyes del Morro

The **Castillo de los Tres Reyes del Morro** ★★ (*$2; every day 9am to 6pm*) was built between 1589 and 1630, around the same time as its mate the Castillo de San Salvador de la Punta. Together the two forts had to defend the entrance of the port from pirate attacks. This magnificent, compact and severe fortress now houses a maritime museum that justifiably gives pride of place to the history of piracy. The lighthouse that casts its long beams of light over the sea and the city was built in 1845 and has not stopped operating since.

When the Castillo del Morro fell into the hands of the British on July 30, 1862, the die was cast for the city. From the moment it was lost, there was nothing to prevent the British army from climbing over the rocky ridge that dominates Havana to the south of Morro and from there blithely bombard the city inside the walls. It was to prevent precisely such a disaster from happening again that the **Fortaleza San Carlos de la Cabaña** ★★★ (*$3; every day 9:30am to 10pm*) was built between 1763 and 1774. The Fortaleza is a very pleasant spot where you can stroll peacefully for hours on end. From the walls of what was one of the most important citadels in the New World, there is a captivating view of the surrounding area, both the Havana side and the Cojimar side, to the west, where the British arrived during the campaign that led to the capture of the city.

Barracks for the thousands of soldiers who were stationed here during the colonial period, the fortress was used as a prison during the 19th century wars of independence and under the dictatorships of Machado and Batista. Many revolutionaries lost their lives here under deplorable conditions. Ernesto Che Guevara established his headquarters here after the fort was taken by the "bearded ones" on January 2, 1959, and a little museum, the **Museo de la Comandancia del Che** ★, recounts this story. This museum holds many documents and photographs from this period and Che's Cuban experience. Several rooms of the fortress are also devoted to the **Museo de la Historia Militar**, which relate the history of the construction of the fort and displays an impressive collection of weapons from all periods.

Every evening at 9pm a strange ceremony is held at the Fortaleza de la Cabaña. From these heights towering over the city, infantrymen dressed in Spanish colours fire a cannon, a ritual reminiscent of the solemn ceremony that in olden days announced the opening and closing of the city gates. Originally there

were two cannon shots, one in the morning and the other in the evening, but the Americans replaced it with a single shot when they took over the city in order to indicate the change of regime.

To visit the two forts, you have to go through the tunnel that goes under the mouth of the bay. You can take a taxi or, if you prefer, one of the many buses that stop in front of the statue of Máximo Gómez right near Castillo de la Punta. Get off at the first stop on the other side of the tunnel, and it is a short walk to either of the two forts.

Casablanca, Regla and Guanabacoa

From the old city, there are several trips you can take to the other side of the bay. The boat crossing is interesting in itself since it gives you a different perspective of the harbour that once made Havana great. The ferries that take passengers across the bay all leave from the same place, Muelle Luz, on Avenida San Pedro, between Calle Santa Clara and Calle Luz. The boats leave the jetty every 10 or 15min and cost just 10 centavos per person.

Exploring

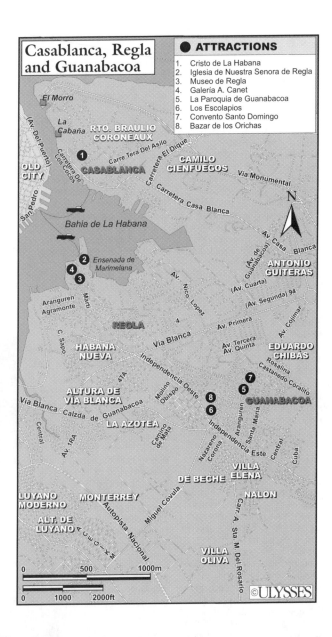

Casablanca, Regla and Guanabacoa

● ATTRACTIONS

1. Cristo de La Habana
2. Iglesia de Nuestra Senora de Regla
3. Museo de Regla
4. Galería A. Canet
5. La Paroquia de Guanabacoa
6. Los Escolapios
7. Convento Santo Domingo
8. Bazar de los Orichas

El Morro

La Cabaña

RTO. BRAULIO CORONEAUX

Carretera De Los Cocos

Carre Tera Del Asilo

Carretera El Dique

CAMILO CIENFUEGOS

Via Monumental

OLD CITY

CASABLANCA

San Pedro

(Av. Del Puerto)

Carretera Casa Blanca

Bahia de La Habana

N

Av. de Casa Blanca

Ensenada de Marimelana

(Av. de Guanabacoa)

ANTONIO GUITERAS

Av. Nico Lopez

(Av. Cuarta)

Aranguren Agramonte

Marti

(Av. Segunda) 94

REGLA

Av. Primera

Av. Colmar

C. Sapo

Via Blanca

Av. Tercera
Av. Quinta

EDUARDO CHIBAS

HABANA NUEVA

Independencia Oeste

Rosalina

Castanedo Coralito

ALTURA DE VIA BLANCA

4TA

Molino Obispo

GUANABACOA

Via Blanca

Calzda de Guanabacoa

LA AZOTEA

Camino de Mata

Independencia Este

Aranguren

Santa Maria

Central

Cuba

Av. 1RA

Nazareno

Corona

VILLA ELENA

DE BECHE

NALON

LUYANO MODERNO

MONTERREY

Autopista Nacional

Miguel Covula

Carr. A. Sta M. Del Rosario

ALT. DE LUYANO

VILLA OLIVA

0   500   1000m

0   1000   2000ft

©ULYSSES

The ferry from **Casablanca** ★ takes you to this peaceful little town from where you can climb up to **Cristo de La Habana**, on the hill that dominates the town. Completed in 1958, the sculpture is of relatively little interest, despite its 18m (59ft) size, but it offers a breathtaking view of the town. There is a little restaurant up there where you can get refreshments and a light meal.

You can also take a ferry to Regla, a historic little town on the other side of the bay, and from there continue on to Guanabacoa, some 5km (3mi) farther. These two towns are renowned for their links with the *santería* cults.

Regla ★ came into being in 1687 with the establishment of a little hermitage that was replaced over the course of the 18th century by **Iglesia de Nuestra Senora de Regla** ★ (*Calle Santuario*), a magnificent church built on a little point that juts out into the bay. Its altarpiece, with its black Virgen de Regla, the patroness of the bay of Havana, is strikingly beautiful.

The **Museo de Regla** ★ (*$2; Mon to Sat 9am to 6pm, Sun 9am to 1pm; Calle Martí, between Calle Factiolo and Calle La Piedra*), located right near the church, is largely devoted to the syncretism that is characteristic of Afro-Cuban religions. Housed in a 19th-century house, it also displays objects from the colonial era, but the rooms devoted to the *orishas* and their cult are the most interesting. The entry price allows you to visit the museum annex, right next to the church.

For those who are interested in contemporary Cuban art, **Galería A. Canet** (*Calle Facciolo no. 167, at the corner of Calle Maceo*) is worth a stop. In a historic house that dates back to 1825, this gallery-studio belonging to artist Antonio Canet, a former member of the Orígenes group, exhibits lithographs and works in acrylic.

From Regla, you can go a little bit farther to the little town of Guanabacoa. Just take the no. 29 bus, which stops in front of the park facing the A. Canet gallery on the corner of Calle Martí and Calle Facciolo, or a tricycle, called a *cyclo*, for $1.

Guanabacoa ★★ seems to have come from another era; its pace is like that of the sleepy little towns on the island. Its colonial character and somewhat dilapidated architecture are evident on every street corner. The centre of the munici-

Exploring

Santería

Santería, the main Afro-Cuban religion, is directly derived from the religion of the Yoruba-speaking people of Nigeria. An animistic religion, *Santería* gives great importance to spirits, here called *Orishas*. At its core, a remarkable syncretism takes place based on similarities found between the spirits of the Yoruban pantheon and Roman Catholic saints. The *Santeros,* masters of ceremonies and soothsayers, are the religious officials, and in Havana, they are treated with the greatest respect by both followers and non-followers.

pality is the Plaza Martí, at the corner of Pepe Antonio and Martí streets. Nearby you will find the old church **La Paroquia de Guanabacoa ★**. Built between 1728 and 1748, both its exterior and its interior are magnificent. The altarpiece and the ceiling are breathtaking.

Two other churches are also worth visiting. **Los Escolapios** (*Calle Máximo Gómez, at the corner of Calle San Antonio*), built toward the end of the 18th century, also has a richly decorated ceiling and gorgeous murals. But the first prize goes to the **Convento Santo Domingo ★★** (*Calle Santo Domingo, at the corner of Calle El Lebredo*). Built

around 1748, this convent church, with its splendid ceilings, stands in front of a square with charming architecture. Occupied by the English in 1762, it played an important role in the history of the town. The saints of the church made life difficult for the invaders by provoking several incidents of a supernatural nature. Guanabacoa was also renowned for the guerilla warfare conducted by the black Creole Pepe Antonio behind enemy lines during the fierce battles that brought the town to its knees.

The town museum is unfortunately closed indefinitely. Two of the rooms devoted to *orichas* that occupied this museum have been transferred to the **Bazar de los Orichas** (*$1; Tue to Sun 9am to 5pm; Calle Martí, between Calle Lama and Calle Cruz Verde*). The entrance fee includes an interesting guided tour that will give you a better understanding of this religious phenomenon that has been spreading like wildfire in Havana for years. The rest of the bazaar consists of a little market that sells very lovely crafts.

To return to Regla to catch the boat, take the no. 28 bus again next to the La Paroquia, or take a tricycle for $1.

Tour B: The Prado and Parque Central

After the old city, the highest concentration of attractions is in the sector stretching from Paseo de Martí, better known as the Prado, to Parque Central. Its history and above all its architecture are from another era and differentiate it clearly from the baroque Havana within the walls. Here the city is neoclassical, with a smattering of Art Nouveau and a smidgin of Art Deco. The whole place has the distinct feeling of a stylized

and highly civilized metropolis.

To get from the grand squares of the old city to this sector, the best thing to do is to take either of the well-travelled Calle Obispo or Calle O'Reilly. These streets lead directly to Parque Central, the heart of the city since the 19th century.

Parque Central

After Old Havana broke the stranglehold of the walls that restrained it, Parque Central became the political and economic centre of the city. With some of the loveliest neocolonial buildings in the city, its large trees and its urban life, this is a particularly pleasant sector. In spite of the sometimes heavy traffic from one part of the park to the other, it never feels congested. The **Estatua de José Martí**, which stands in the middle of the park, was erected in 1905 and is the oldest statue of Martí on the island of Cuba.

Of all the buildings surrounding the park, the most beautiful is probably the **Palacio del Centro Gallego** ★★, home to the **Gran Teatro de La Habana** (*$2; every day 9am to 6pm; Paseo*

Exploring

Calle O'Reilly

One might well ask how one of Havana's main streets has come to be called O'Reilly. This thoroughfare is named for Alexander O'Reilly, an Irish soldier born in Dublin in 1725, who joined the Spanish army at the early age of 10. As an officer, he accompanied the Conde de Ricla when he took back Havana from the British, as a result of the Treaty of Paris in 1763. An expert in fortifications, O'Reilly took part in the planning and construction of Fortaleza de San Carlos de La Cabaña. Before he died in 1794, he was given the title of Conde de O'Reilly. The O'Reilly clan quickly became one of the most prosperous and powerful families in the colony.

de Martí, on the corner of Calle San Rafael). Bearing witness to the liveliness of the Spanish community after the expulsion of Spain, the Galician centre opened its doors in 1915 and has been a cultural beacon on the island since. It is especially prominent in the area of dance, and the National Ballet of Cuba has taken up residence there. The building's style is definitely eclectic, a tasteful blend of neoclassicism, Art Nouveau, French Renaissance and Rococo. The interior is as incredible as the exterior.

Right next to the Centro Gallego, on the other side of Calle San Rafael, is another jewel of Havana neoclassical architecture, the **Hotel Inglaterra**. Completed in 1875, it was the first luxury hotel in the city. In this case, its warm, brightly coloured interior is in sharp contrast with its severe exterior. The style here is clearly Andalusian, with its blue *azulejos* (tiles) which create an utterly charming effect.

From the other side of the park, there are two magnificent buildings in a more formal neoclassical stye. **Manzana de Gómez**, completed in 1910, stands on Calle Agramonte between

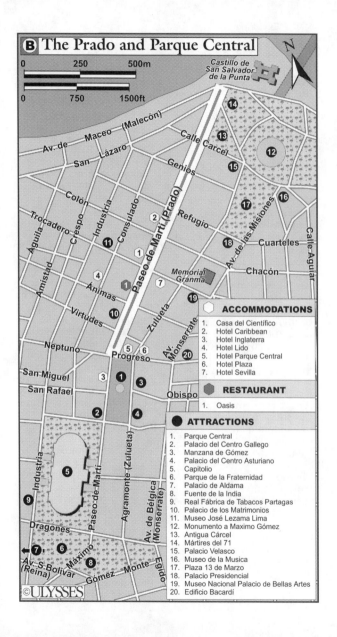

B The Prado and Parque Central

0 — 250 — 500m

0 — 750 — 1500ft

N

Castillo de San Salvador de la Punta

Av. de Maceo (Malecón)

San Lázaro

Calle Cárcel

Genios

Colón

Trocadero

Crespo

Industria

Consulado

Paseo de Martí (Prado)

Refugio

Av. de las Misiones

Cuarteles

Calle Aguiar

Aguila

Amistad

Animas

Virtudes

Chacón

Memorial Granma

Zulueta

Neptuno

Av. Monserrate

San Miguel

San Rafael

Progreso

Obispo

Industria

Paseo de Martí

Agramonte (Zulueta)

Av. Bélgica (Monserrate)

Egido

Dragones

Av. S-Bolívar (Reina)

Máximo

Gómez

Monte

©ULYSSES

ACCOMMODATIONS

1. Casa del Científico
2. Hotel Caribbean
3. Hotel Inglaterra
4. Hotel Lido
5. Hotel Parque Central
6. Hotel Plaza
7. Hotel Sevilla

RESTAURANT

1. Oasis

ATTRACTIONS

1. Parque Central
2. Palacio del Centro Gallego
3. Manzana de Gómez
4. Palacio del Centro Asturiano
5. Capitolio
6. Parque de la Fraternidad
7. Palacio de Aldama
8. Fuente de la India
9. Real Fábrica de Tabacos Partagas
10. Palacio de los Matrimonios
11. Museo José Lezama Lima
12. Monumento a Maximo Gómez
13. Antigua Cárcel
14. Mártires del 71
15. Palacio Velasco
16. Museo de la Musica
17. Plaza 13 de Marzo
18. Palacio Presidencial
19. Museo Nacional Palacio de Bellas Artes
20. Edificio Bacardí

Calle Obispo and Calle Progreso. During the first years of the 20th century, this building housed a vast market. It is still home to numerous stores, none of which, unfortunately, are particularly interesting. The interior of the building is disappointing.

From the other side of Obispo, still on Agramonte, the grand **El Palacio del Centro Asturiano** ★ is striking. An enormous neoclassical building whose four towers seem to touch the sky, it was opened in 1928. Until quite recently, it housed the country's Supreme Court. Although the building is currently under renovation, you can still get a sense of its monumental exterior, with its magnificent sculptures.

Lantern, Palacio de Aldama

The north of Parque Central seems to be on the verge of a hotel boom, with three of the most beautiful hotels in the city open or about to open. The south opens onto one of the largest buildings in the city, the Capitolio.

★★

The Capitolio and the Parque de la Fraternidad

Opened in 1929 by dictator Gerardo Machado, the **Capitolio** ★★★ *($3; every day 9am to 8pm; Paseo de Martí, between Avenida Dragones and Calle San Martín)* was the seat of the Senate and the House of Representatives until the revolution of 1959. Inspired by the Capitol in Washington as well as the basilica of Saint-Pierre-de-Rome and the Invalides in Paris, the building is remarkable for its size. You only have to climb up the steps, flanked by two huge bronze statues by the Italian artist Zanelli to feel overwhelmed by the sheer mass of the place. Today, the lower and higher floors are used as offices and conference halls by the Ministry of Science and Technology. The middle floor is, however, open to the public. A guided tour is definitely worthwhile, as a glance at the interior will convinced you. The huge 17m (55ft) statue of the Republic, the third largest interior bronze statue in the world, is only one of its superlative surprises.

The **Parque de la Fraternidad**, at the end of the Prado, was named soon after the Panamerican Conference, held in Havana in 1928. At that time a tree was planted in its centre in a mixture of soil from all the countries that sent delegates to the conference. The tree is still there, surrounded by a high black fence. The park has become an important crossroads for the city's public transportation, and all the buses seem to converge on it. It is an interesting place, albeit a bit noisy.

On the west side of the park, on Calle Amistad at the corner of Avenida Simón Bolívar, there is magnificent building that is worth a detour. The **Palacio de Aldama** ★ is considered one of the most beautiful examples of neoclassical architecture in the city. Built between 1840 and 1845, the palace was the property of the Aldama family until 1870. In that year, its owner, Miguel Aldama was accused of conspiracy, and the palace was confiscated. Aldama fled to the United States to collect money to sustain the rebel forces in the east. Since then it fulfilled several functions before being turned into an office building. Today it houses the monument division of the cultural heritage department. Although theoretically it is not open to the public, even a look at its massive exterior and its entrance, flanked by two enormous lamps, is worthwhile.

On the other side of the park stands **Fuente de la India**, one of Havana's enduring symbols. Made of white marble by Italian sculptor Giuseppe Gaggini, this fountain is a little removed from everything, as if it were lost in the middle of the noise and exhaust fumes.

Finally, it seems that one cannot visit Havana without taking an interest in the cigars that derive their name from the city. Just behind the Capitolio is one of the city's large cigar manufacturers, **Real Fábrica de Tabacos Partagas** (*$10; Mon to Sat 9am to 5pm; Calle Industria no. 520, between Calle Dragones and Calle Barcelona*). Founded in 1845, it is open to the public for a modest contribution of $10! Your choice.

★★

The Prado

The Prado, or Paseo de Martí, inaugurated in 1772 under the name of the Alameda de Extramuros,

Exploring

became the major prome-
nade in Havana in the 19th
century. Bourgeois houses
sprang up on both sides of
the central lane, reflecting
the new wealth brought by
sugar-cane cultivation. In its
present incarnation, which
goes back to 1928, it is one
of the most attractive places
in the city. If you sit on
one of the stone benches in
the shade of the tall trees,
you're sure to meet people.

Few of the lovely houses
that line the promenade are
open to the public. The
Palacio de los Matrimonios ★
(*Prado no. 302, between Calle
Ánimas and Virtudes*) is only
open on Saturdays for civil
weddings, but it is worth
the effort to go there. The
house in which the Palacio
is located was built in 1914
to house the Spanish ca-
sino, another indication of
the continuing opulence of
the Spanish community
after the proclamation of
the Republic. The third
floor has to be seen to be
believed. With its richly
decorated ceiling and its
paintings with historical
themes, its magnificence is
unparalleled.

Although it is technically in
the Centro, the **Museo José
Lezama Lima** ★ (*$2; Tue to
Sat 9am to 5pm, Sun 9am to
1pm; Calle Trocadero no. 162,
between Calle Industria and
Calle Consulado*) is men-
tioned here because of its

proximity. This little museum will appeal to those
interested in Cuban literature and art in general. Located in the little rooms the
writer occupied for 49 years
from 1927 to 1976, the year
of his death, the museum
displays personal objects
that belonged to this genius
of letters and also most of
the art works he owned in
his lifetime. A great retro-
spective of Cuban modern
art.

To the north, the Prado
leads to the famous
Malecón, right near the
Fortaleza San Carlos de la
Cabaña. A series of parks
opens out on the right,
where the enormous
Monumento de Maximo Gómez
sits imposingly. Originally
Dominican, he fought be-
side the Cuban rebels during the two wars of inde-
pendence in the 19th cen-
tury and was, with Martí
and Maceo, largely responsible for the victory over
Spain. From this monument
there is an unrestricted view
of the presidential palace.

On the west side of the
parks, you can still see the
remains of **Antigua Cárcel de
La Habana**, a prison built in
1835 to rid the Palacio de
Los Capitanes Generales of
its undesirable guests.
When it was built, it was
the largest prison in Latin
America. One of its walls
was used to construct the

Mártires del 71, the monument raised to the memory of the medical students who were executed here for having desecrated the tomb of the owner of a pro-Spanish newspaper (see "Portrait," p 22).

Right at the corner of Calle Zulueta and Calle Cárcel stands one of the most beautiful Art Nouveau buildings in the capital, the **Palacio Velasco**. Built in 1912, the palace is now occupied by the Spanish Embassy.

On the other side, at the corner of Avenida de las Misiones, the **Museo de la Música ★** (*$2; Mon to Sat 9am to 5pm; Calle Capdevila no. 1, between Calle Habana and Calle Aguiar*) is definitely worth visiting. Established in an old house that dates back to the beginning of the 20th century, the museum will give you an excellent overview of the evolution of Cuban music and the groups that made it famous. Particularly interesting is the Fernando Ortiz room, which was named after the renowned Cuban anthropologist and displays a large number of Afro-Cuban percussion instruments that were part of his private collection.

Between the Palacio Velasco and the Museo de la Música extends the **Plaza 13 de Marzo**, which is named

in memory of the assault by the Directorio Revolucionario on the presidential palace on March 13, 1957. The Plaza looks directly out onto the **Palacio Presidencial ★★★**, a magnificent, eclectic building that once more marries neoclassicism with Art Nouveau. Many political figures have addressed the inhabitants of Havana from its balcony, from Grau San Martín to Fidel Castro. Built between 1913 and 1920, the palace is now home to the **Museo de la Revolución** (*$3; every day 10am to 5pm; Calle Refugio no.1, between Avenida de las Misiones and Calle Zulueta*), a flawless museum that occupies the most beautiful rooms in this magnificent building. It is definitely worth a visit. Retracing the long path travelled by the revolutionary elements of Cuban society up to Batista's final overthrow in the first few days of 1959, the exhibit is illustrated with numerous newspaper cuttings, documents and objects ranging from an anonymous pocket knife to a stuffed mullet belonging to Che. This museum is an essential stop for anyone interested in the history of Cuba.

Part of the museum, the **Memorial Granma** displays the yacht that sailed Castro and his 81 companions from Mexico to Cuba in

Exploring

The Attack on the Presidential Palace

On March 13, 1957, an important event in the Cuban revolutionary struggle took place. At 3pm, a commando of the Directorio Revolucionario, led by José Antonio Echeverría, attacked the Palacio Presidencial. The aim of this offensive was to put an abrupt end to Dictator Fulgencio Batista's days in office. Contrary to the M-26-7 of Castro, who held the view that only a long-term guerrilla war could bring the dictatorship to an end, the Directorio wanted to topple the regime by removing its ruler.

Both well organized and armed, the commando was divided into three groups. The first was to attack the Palacio Presidencial, go to Batisita's office on the first floor and do away with him. At the same time, a second group led by Echeverría himself, was to occupy the radio station CMQ and announce Batista's death. This news, they hoped, would pro-

voke the people to rise up against the police. And finally, the third group was to take up positions on the roofs of the Palacio de Arte, Hotel Sevilla-Biltmore and various other buildings around the palace in order to prevent or delay the arrival of reinforcements.

The plan was based on three assumptions: one, that Batista would be in the executive office on the first floor; two, that the dictator's personal guards could be taken by surprise and easily overcome; and three, that the communications centre on the ground floor could be destroyed during the first minutes of the attack. The events did not go as planned. The 50-some people who took part in the assault lost the surprise advantage right from the start and the soldiers' resistance was stronger than anticipated. The attackers were not able to prevent a message from being sent for reinforcements, which had disastrous consequences. And to top it all off, Batista was not where they anticipated he would be at the time of the offensive: he was in his small private office on the second floor near his residential quarters. Unable to take Batista, the palace attack collapsed and ended in an absolute blood bath. Echeverría lost his life, as did most of the assailants: the soldiers showed no mercy during or after the attack.

Batista's response to this assassination attempt was bloody and it left the Directorio Revolucionario's urban revolutionary force in a state of complete disorganization. From this moment on, there was nothing and nobody to contest Fidel Castro and his M-26-7 at the head of the revolutionary movement. Although the attack was unsuccessful, it did, at least, have the effect of breaking the myth of invulnerability surrounding Batista. It was clear to everyone that only chance had saved him from death. It is even said that from this moment on, the *Santeros* changed their views, convinced that the *Orichas* would no longer protect the dictator.

1956. The boat is encased in a strange glass box around which various other symbols of the civil war are haphazardly arranged. To get to the memorial go through the Museo de la Revolución.

The **Museo Nacional de Bellas Artes** ★★★ *($3; Thu to Mon 10am to 5pm; Calle Trocadero, between Zulueta and Montserrate, ☎62-1643)* is the country's main museum of fine arts and an absolute must-see. It exhibits a large number of works by local artists and houses the most extensive collection of Greek and Roman ceramics in Latin America. The colonial gallery is essentially devoted to 19th-century Cuban landscapes, and prints from the same era offer a glimpse of what the city looked like and how its inhabitants lived. A number of works from the 16th century are also on display. Make sure to take a look at the 18th-century prints by José Nicolas de Escalera, considered the first Cuban painter, and even more importantly, those by Vicente Escobar. The latter was the most celebrated artist of his time, for he was the official painter of the Captains-General, and painted local notables. According to legend, Vicente Escobar was Goya's protégé during his stay in Spain, although there are no documents to support that theory. The contemporary Cuban gallery is not to be missed. If you are interested in paintings produced since the *vanguardia* in 1920, your attention will surely be drawn to the works of Raúl Martinez. Adopting the pop art style inspired by Andy Warhol, Martinez searched the popular imagination of the Revolution for his images. The painting of Che and the principal figures of the Revolution (Castro, Maceo, Martí, Cienfuegos) is superb.

The museum is unfortunately closed for renovations. If all goes according to plan, it should reopen in early 2001.

Down Avenida Monserrate, just before Calle O'Reilly at the end of the old walls, stands one of the most interesting buildings in the city, the **Edificio Bacardí** ★ (*Avenida de Bélgica no. 261, at the corner of Calle San Juan de Dios*). Built in 1930, this splendid Art Deco building contrasts starkely with its surroundings. It is presently occupied by the headquarters of foreign companies involved in various projects and is being completely renovated. You can go in to look at the entrance hall, and on the second floor, on the right as you enter, there is a small café-bar, which used to be a private bar. Open from Monday to Friday, 8am to 8pm, this little bar is the perfect place to have a drink at the end of the day or a quick meal.

Tour C: The Centro

To some, the Centro is just a cumbersome space between the old city and the Vedado. It is, however, one of the best places to get an idea of what Cuban life is really like. The heart of Havana beats here at its own pace and the feeling is quite different from that of Habana Vieja. It can be very pleasant to stroll about in this lively neighbourhood.

The Centro is generally considered to be the area bordered to the east by the Prado and the Capitolio and to the west by the Calzada de Infanta. It does not have any particularly interesting

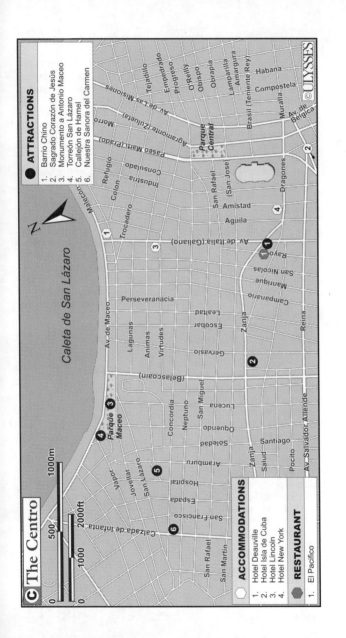

C The Centro

ATTRACTIONS

1. Barrio Chino
2. Sagrado Corazón de Jesús
3. Monumento a Antonio Maceo
4. Torreón San Lázaro
5. Callejón de Hamel
6. Nuestra Señora del Carmen

ACCOMMODATIONS

1. Hotel Deauville
2. Hotel Isla de Cuba
3. Hotel Lincoln
4. Hotel New York

RESTAURANT

1. El Pacifico

© ULYSSES

Caleta de San Lázaro

Parque Central

Parque Maceo

architecture. At one time the commercial centre of the city, the Centro includes certain arteries that have kept the traces of their mercantile past. Under the Republic, the **Calle San Rafael** was the Centro's shopping street. A pedestrian way, it starts between the Hotel Inglaterra and the Gran Teatro and continues up to Calle Galiano. There is not much to buy, but it is interesting to see these store-window displays from the 1940s and 1950s with American brands and neon signs.

Calle Galiano, also called Avenida de Italia, extends Calle San Rafael a short way. If you head south along it, you will approach the **Barrio Chino** (*Calle Cuchillo, entre Calle San Nicolás et Calle Rayo*). The Chinese quarter of Havana is but a shadow of its former self, the majority of the Chinese having left the city in the 1960s, but the area still has its charms. Now just a street lined with restaurants and a little market, under the Batista regime it was an important distribution centre for erotic films. The Pacífico restaurant, at the bottom of Cuchillo on San Nicolás, was one of the capital's livelier night spots.

Calle Galiano, on one corner of Calle Cuchillo, is crossed by Avenida Zanja. This street comes out to the east on Calle Dragones, the street that separates the Parque de la Fraternidad from the Capitolio.

To cross the Centro and get from the old city to Vedado, you have several options. Many streets traverse the entire length of the Centro, such as Calle Virtudes, or street of virtue, well known for the number and quality of its brothels in the 1950s. Otherwise, you can always go alongside the central district by slipping along its flanks, either on Avenida Simón Bolívar, or the Malecón.

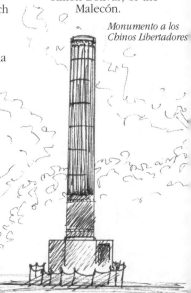

Monumento a los Chinos Libertadores

The Chinese in Havana

It is estimated that between 1844 and 1874, some 150,000 Chinese were brought to the island of Cuba as contractual workers to replace the black workforce, which had become very costly because of British opposition to the slave trade. The Chinese were generally under contract for a period of eight years, after which many chose to settle here permanently. The Chinese community in Havana soon formed the core of this diaspora.

Almost exclusively from the Canton area in southern China, the first wave of Chinese immigrants was soon joined by a second wave, less numerous but wealthier. They came from the west coast of the United States in response to this new offer of work. In the 1870s, the first Chinese businesses in Havana appeared and with time, the Chinese community gained some notoriety.

Of the 25,000 Chinese in Cuba in 1960, 12,000 of them lived in the capital. Following the Revolution, many of the richest Chinese left the city for other havens, leaving behind only a few restaurants and traces of an unusual adventure.

In the Vedado, there is a strange monument dedicated to the Chinese who died during the wars of independence against Spain. Erected in 1931, the Monumento a los Chinos Libertadores is inscribed in both Spanish and Chinese with these words by Gonzalo de Quesada, a relative of Martí: "*There was not one Chinese-Cuban deserter; there was not one Chinese-Cuban traitor!*"

Exploring

Avenida Simón Bolívar is noisy and the exhaust fumes are unpleasantly concentrated here, but a walk along this avenue will take you to the neogothic church **Sagrado Corazón de Jesús** (*Avenida Simón Bolívar, between Calle Gervasio and Calle Padre Valera*). This route will get you to the Quinta de los Molinos, just behind the university.

The **Malecón** ★★, on the other side of the Centro, is a much more pleasant way of going from the old city to Vedado. Following the ocean along this boulevard, which is the pride of Havanans, could turn out to be a unique experience. Not only is the view stunning and the sunsets spellbinding, but the air is good and there is plenty of life. Constructed at the beginning of the 20th century, the Malecón extends for about 12km (7mi) from the old city at the chateau de la Chorrera to the mouth of the Río Almendares. The most typical section is the one that extends from the Prado to Parque Antonio Maceo, at the gates of Vedado. There you will see lovely pastel-coloured houses that face the sea and give the boulevard a kind of gentleness, which it gradually loses farther west.

The **Parque Maceo** is too noisy and too busy to be relaxing, but the **Monumento a Antonio Maceo**, built to commemorate the mulatto general known as the "Bronze Titan," is quite good. At the far west of the park stands the little **Torreón San Lázaro**. Erected in the 17th century, it served as a look-out post in the era when pirates were everywhere up and down the coast.

From there, you can continue on the Malecón as far as La Rampa, the main artery of the Vedado, or you can take San Lázaro, which will take you up to the main entrance to the Universidad de La Habana (University of Havana). Students marched down this street in the thousands to protest against the various regimes and their policies during the turbulent years of the Republic. If you take the latter, make sure to stop at the **Callejón de Hamel** ★. This little street that runs parallel to Calle San Lázaro, between Calle Hospital and Calle Aramburu, is a real temple to Afro-Cuban culture. Since 1990, people have been busy painting vast murals on the walls of the surrounding houses and decorating them with sculptures that are almost animist. There is even a little shrine to the *santería* cult. A few interesting art galleries seem to be flourishing on the street, and on Sundays the sounds of the Afro-Cuban rumba, a hymn to the African presence on the island, can be heard from noon to the end of the day.

Before you get to the university, on Calzada de Infanta at the corner of Calle Neptuno two streets east of San Lázaro, you will see the magnificent church **Nuestra Senora del Carmen ★**. It would be difficult to miss, with its enormous 60m (200ft) column supporting a 7.5m (25ft) bronze of the virgin Mary weighing more than 9 tonnes. The interior is absolutely beautiful. Built in 1925, its interior decoration includes 10 altarpieces made of coloured tiles, which date back to the 18th century and were salvaged from the old Iglesia de San Felipe in the old city. The overall effect is spectacular.

Tour D: The Vedado

Until the second half of the 19th century, the Vedado was just a wooded hill surrounded by enormous haciendas. The organization of the whole area into residential districts did not begin until the 1860s. But it was really not until the arrival of the Americans, at the beginning of the 20th century, that it was turned into a chic neighbourhood full of magnificent residences and hotels towering above the city, a reminder of the good old days of American gambling and tourism.

Vedado's main artery, Calle 23, also called **La Rampa,** goes from the Malecón to the Cementerio de Colón, and it is cut across by two large avenues, Avenida G (Avenida de los Presidente) and Paseo. By taking the former, you will get to Quinta de los Molinos, while the latter is a pleasant alternative that takes you to the heart of the Plaza de la Revolución. The majority of the hotels, restaurants and office buildings are located between Calle 17 and Calle 27 on one side, and Calle J to Malecón on the other.

To get an idea of the wealth that existed in Havana in the beginning of the 20th century, just walk a little way along Calle 17. The grandiose houses that you see, for the most part built in the 1920s, evoke the opulence that followed the explosion in sugar prices after the First World War. Few of them, however, are officially open to the public. Nevertheless, there are a few that house public organizations, so you can have a look. One of these is the **Casa de ICAP**, between Calle H and Calle I; another is the house of the **Unión de Escritores y Artistas de Cuba,** at

Exploring

the corner of Calle H, both open from 8:30am to 8pm. Farther on, you can visit the **Casa de la Amistad** (*Tue to Sat 9:30am to midnight; Paseo no. 406, between Calle 17 and Calle 19*) with no problem. A superb house built in 1925 by Senator Juan Pedro Barro for his wife, the Casa de la Amistad was recently converted into a restaurant-bar, *tienda* and concert hall complex. The **Museo Nacional de Arte Decorativo** ★ (*$2; Tue to Sat 11am to 6:30; Calle 17 no. 507, corner of Calle E*) is also located in a magnificent home built at the beginning of the 20th century. The house itself is as worthwhile as the collection of decorative-art objects exhibited there.

The Malecón, from La Rampa to Rió Almendares

The vestiges of U.S. predominance over Havana are legion in Vedado. You only have to look at the large hotels established in high towers in one part of La Rampa or another to understand that this presence was more than symbolic. One flamboyant sign of this domination is the **Habana Libre**, at the corner of Calle

---

● ATTRACTIONS

1. Casa de l'ICAP
2. Unión de Escritores y Artistas de Cuba
3. Casa de la Amistad
4. Museo Nacional de Arte Decorativo
5. Monumento a las Victimas del Maine
6. U.S. Interests Section
7. Monumento a Calixto García
8. Castillo de Santa Dorotea de la Luna de Chorrera (R)
9. Plaza Ignacio-Agramonte and Museo Antropológico Montané snd Museo de Historia Natural Felipe Poey

10. Museo Napoleónico
11. Monumento a Julio Antonio Mella
12. Museo Casa Abel Santamaría
13. Quinta de los Molinos
14. Plaza de la Revolución
15. Monumento a José Martí
16. Museo Postal Cubano
17. Cementario Cristóbal Colón

(R) Property with Restaurant (see description)

◯ ACCOMMODATIONS

1. Colina
2. Hotel Bruzon
3. Hotel Melia Cohiba
4. Hotel Nacional
5. Hotel Presidente
6. Habana Riviera

● RESTAURANTS

1. Castillo de Jagüa
2. Cinecitta
3. Doña Yulla et Taberna Don Pepe
4. El Cochinito
5. 1813
6. Restaurante Pekin

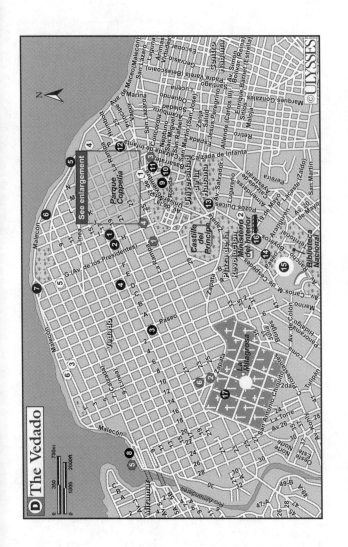

D The Vedado

N

See enlargement

Parque Coppelia

Malecón

Malecón

Vedado

Malecón

Miramar

Río Almendares

© ULYSSES

23 and Calle L, formerly the Havana Hilton and the highest building in the city. Another is the **Capri**, at the corner of Calle 21 and Calle N, the centre of the American mafia in Cuba, whose large casino formerly occupied the Salón Rojo to the right of the main entrance. The U.S. presence is still felt all along this part of Malecón, which goes from La Rampa to the small fortress La Chorrera at the mouth of the Río Almendares.

Upper-class Vedado residence

If you follow the Malecón to the end of Calle 17, starting from the **Hotel Nacional**, you will immediately see the **Monumento a las Victimas del Maine**, inaugurated in 1925. The two columns that form the backbone of the monument formerly supported an eagle, whose wings can be seen at the Museo de la Ciudad. Two bronze plaques are fixed to each part of the monument; one lists the names of the people who disappeared in this tragedy (see "Portrait," p 25), while the other, added after the revolution, rededicates the monument to the "the victims of the *Maine*, who were sacrificed by the greed of imperialism in its attempt to take control of the island of Cuba."

A little farther west is the **U.S. Interests Section** (of the Swiss Embassy), which serves in place of the embassy that was closed down with the cutting of diplomatic ties between the two countries. The concrete building is well guarded (do not try to take photographs or hang around the vicinity). Here, distrust of Cubans is at its most profound. Just in front of this building, which officially houses the Swiss embassy, there is a large square that is used as a gathering point for large anti-imperialist demonstrations.

Farther still, at the end of Calle G, stands the **Monumento a Calixto García**. In several ways, this magnificent monument is indicative of the animosity that divides the Cubans and Americans. It recalls the affront of the United States to General Cubain, who, after having taken part in the landing of Yankee troops in Santiago de Cuba (with a certain lack of enthusiasm, it is true), was then refused entrance to the city once it had been liberated. A series of 32 bronze plaques that surround the monument tell the story, in pictures, of the participation of General Cubain in the 19th century wars of independence.

At the end of Paseo, another magnificent street lined with trees and some fantastic houses, the **Hotel Riviera ★** is perhaps the most beautiful monument to U.S. presence in Cuba. The flower of Meyer Lansky's gambling empire, no place in Havana retains better the atmosphere of the 1950s, when gangsters ran the show. The decor is faithful to the period when it was designed, and it takes us directly back to this troubled period that gave the city its sad fame.

From the Hotel Riviera, you can keep going on the Malecón to the Río Almendares, and finish exploring the Malecón on a more colonial note with a visit to the **Castillo de Santa Dorotea de Luna de Chorrera ★**. This guard

post, built in 1646, was built on the little bay that opens out onto the mouth of the river to protect the rear of the city. This place is ravishing, and you can have a drink or a meal on the terrace that has recently been built at its base.

The Universidad de La Habana

The Universidad de La Habana was for a long time the centre of opposition to the dictatorial regimes of the Republic. Its atmosphere is now calmer, but some signs of this explosive period still remain. The university, which is closed on the weekends, is worth a visit not only for its museums, but also for its grandiose neocolonial architecture.

The best way to reach the university is to take **Calle San Lázaro**, the street that was regularly used by the students for their huge demonstrations. This route takes you right to the front of the monumental 163-step staircase, the Escalita, at the top of which sits an immense statue of the Alma Mater. The **Plaza Ignacio-Agramonte** is the heart of the campus. It extends behind the monumental neoclassical gate built of four Corinthian

Exploring

columns that tower over the staircase. Dating back to the beginning of the 20th century, this is the oldest part of the university. The square is surrounded by four magnificent buildings that are occupied by the rector's office, the faculty of law, the faculty of sciences and the library.

The Plaza Ignacio-Agramonte also houses two museums that are worth mentioning: the **Museo Antropológico Montané** and the **Museo de Historia Natural Felipe Poey**.

The **Museo Antropológico Montané** *($1; Mon to Fri 9am to noon and 1pm to 4pm; Edificio Felipe Poey, Plaza Ignacio Agramonte, Universidad de La Habana,* ☎*79-3488)* houses the most extensive assortment of pre-Columbian artifacts in the country, including a collection of Taino art featuring coral sculptures and the Idol of Bayamo, the first piece of 17th-century indigenous art discovered. The Tobacco Idol, a wooden sculpture with shells for eyes, is definitely the most popular piece in this little museum. Natural history lovers can stop in at the **Museo de Historia Natural Felipe Poey** *($1; Mon to Fri 9am to noon and 1pm to 4pm)*, located in the courtyard of the same building.

Right nearby, the **Museo Napoleónico** ★ *($1; Tue to Sat 10am to 5:30pm, Sun 9am to 12:30pm; Calle San Miguel no. 1159, at the corner of Ronda,* ☎*79-1460)*, housed in a Florentine-style palace, displays articles that once belonged to Napoleon Bonaparte. It is considered one of the most important museums of its kind in the world. What is the largest collection of Napoleon's belongings in the Americas doing in Havana? Multimillionaire Julio Lobo, the richest man in Cuba before the Revolution and a great admirer of Napoleon, purchased these pieces in Europe, mainly in France. They include a lamp Napoleon gave to Josephine, several pieces of furniture, porcelain figurines, bronzes, pistols, telescopes and various other objects used by the former Emperor of France. The multimillionaire's sumptuous home is worth a visit in itself, especially the fourth floor, with its lavish library containing over 4,000 books on Napoleon. Unfortunately, you cannot handle the books without obtaining special permission beforehand.

Right in front of the main entrance to the university stands the **Monumento a Julio Antonio Mella**, a monument in memeory of the student leader and founder of the Cuban Communist Party

Humboldt 7

During the 1950s, members of the urban guerrilla force were most at ease working in the Vedado, and it was here that they took refuge when they found themselves in difficulty. So during the days following the bloody attack on the Palacio Presidencial, four survivors, two of whom were leaders of the Directorio Revolucionario, went to Calle Humboldt number 7, one street east of La Rampa right next to the Malecón, to escape the police searches. This apartment had been found by Marcos Rodríguez, a theatre student at the University of Havana. What the fugitives did not know was that this "Marquitos" was also a member of the Juventud Socialista, the young socialists.

At the time, the Cuban Socialist Party had made a decision that would have grave consequences: unable to take control of the revolutionary forces that were quietly assuming the lead in the war against the island's capitalist regime, the party decided to eliminate its rivals. So, on April 20, 1957, young Rodríguez gave the police the address of the apartment where the survivors of March 13 were hiding, sending them to a certain death. It took only minutes to find and kill the four men, thus leaving the Directorio Revolucionario leaderless.

Exploring

and a symbol of the importance of the student movements in the struggle for freedom in Cuba. In 1923, before founding the Communist party (1925), Mella formed the Federación Estudiantil Universitaria, the protest organization that spearheaded the vast opposition movement that came to life in the 1920s. Forced into exile in 1927, he left Havana for Mexico, where he continued to plan an insurrection against the dictator Gerardo Machado. The latter unfortunately beat him to it and had him assassinated in January 1929. This savage act inflamed the university community and provoked the first convulsions of the Revolution of the 1930s, which finally forced the tyrant out.

The **Museo Casa Abel Santamaría** ★ (*free admission; Mon to Fri 9am to 5pm, Sat 9am to 1pm; Calle 25 no. 174, apartment 601-603, between Calle O and Calle Infanta*) is another remnant of university unrest in the years preceding the Revolution. The museum occupies a small apartment which, after the coup of 1952, became a sort of general headquarters for the revolutionary student forces. Through his contacts with the student representatives, Abel Santamaría, a former student of the Universidad de La Habana and subsequently an accountant for the Havana branch of the auto manufacturer Pontiac, joined up with a young lawyer named Fidel Castro, to whom he lent these two little rooms to organize the armed struggle. The attack on the Moncada barracks, which cost the young Santamaría his life, was organized here.

Behind the university is a pleasant little park that is a good place for a little rest.

The **Quinta de los Molinos** ★ (*$1; Tue to Sat 9am to 5pm, Sun 9am to 1pm; Avenida Salvador Allende, at the corner of Calle G*) is the home of the **Museo Máximo Gómez**. The museum is unfortunately closed for renovation, but the outside of the house and the park surrounding it are worth a visit. Built in the 1830s (the second floor was probably added in 1848), the house was at that time located on the south side of the wooded hill that was still part of Vedado at that time. It was the residence of one of the colonels-in-chief of the colony, who fled there to escape the torrid air of the old city during the gruelling days of the hot season. Máximo Gómez actually only stayed there for three months after the capitulation of the Spanish forces, while the United States was wondering what to do with this incumbent general, but his name remains linked to this place.

The Plaza de la Revolución

Construction of the Plaza de la Revolución (previously called the Plaza Cívica) began under the rule of Batista. Huge demonstrations by the masses are organized there periodi cally, the largest on July 26, the date of the attack on the Moncada barracks. Otherwise, it has the atmosphere of a vast deserted parking lot.

The Plaza is dominated by the enormous **Monumento a José Martí ★**. Consisting of a tower some 140m (460ft) high that supports an enormous statue of the national hero, there are three rooms at the base of the monument that are open to the public. Two of them are dedicated to the life and works of the revolutionary and the third describes the history of the Monumento and the square in which it is located. From the top of the tower there is a fantastic view of Havana. The memorial and the observation tower are open from Monday to Friday between 9:30am and 5:30pm. It costs $3 to visit the rooms at the foot of the monument, and $5 if you also want to avail yourself of the view offered by the observation tower. The square is flanked to the east by the National Library, the Ministry of Defense and the head offices of *Granma*, the official

newspaper of the Communist Party of Cuba; to the south by the austere Party headquarters, and to the north by the Ministry of the Interior, whose facade features an enormous portrait of Che Guevara.

Opposite the bus station stands the uninviting Ministry of Communications. Inside, the **Museo Postal Cubano** *($1; Mon to Fri 9am to 4pm; Avenida Independencia and 19 de Mayo, ☎57-4021)* displays a large collection of old stamps and recounts the history of the Cuban mail service.

Cementerio Cristobal Colon

Undoubtedly the loveliest cemetery in Cuba and one of the most famous in all of Latin America, the immense **Cementerio Cristóbal Colón** *(Calle 12, at the corner of Avenida 23)* was laid out in 1876. It contains over 800,000 graves, and many of the tombstones are veritable works of art by such famous

Plaza de la Revolución

Exploring

sculptors as Saavedra and Ramos Blancos. Take a bike ride or a walk through the cemetery to discover how truly magnificent it is. Don't be surprised to find little handcrafted dolls scattered on the ground near some of the tombstones; many locals carry out Afro-Cuban religious rituals here. The dolls and scraps of colourful cloth are *trabajos*, offerings made to various deities so that they will grant the supplicant's wishes.

Ask for directions to the grave of **La Milagrosa** (the Miraculous Woman), where many Catholics go to leave offerings or ask for blessings. According to legend, the woman in question died while she was pregnant and was buried while the fetus was still alive. The tomb was apparently opened, and the baby was found in its mother's arms.

At the entrance to the cemetery there is a small market, some pleasant restaurants and a few cinemas, including the well-known Cine Chaplin. The atmosphere is interesting and it is well worth a few moments of your visit.

Tour E: Miramar

Miramar is Havana's most chic neighbourhood. Many of the area's beautiful colonial-style houses were abandoned by Cubans who fled the country when Fidel Castro came to power in 1959. They have since become the homes of prominent members of the regime, or have been converted into embassies, local offices of foreign companies

● ATTRACTIONS

1. La Maison
2. Acuario Nacional de Cuba
3. Maqueta de La Habana
4. Russian Enbassy
5. Puente de Hierro

◯ ACCOMMODATIONS

1. Chateau Miramar
2. Hotel Copacabana
3. Hotel Icemar
4. Hotel Mirazul
5. Hotel Neptuno et Hotel Triton
6. Hotel Villamar
7. Melia-Habana
8. Novotel Miramar
9. Residencia Universitaria Ispaje

◆ RESTAURANTS

1. Don Cangrejo
2. Dos Gardenias, Gambinas, Shangai
3. El Ajibe
4. El Tocororo
5. Le Sélect
6. Lisboa
7. Quinta y 16
8. Vistamar

The colonial architecture of the old city is enlivened by the lovely spots residents have created for themselves.
- *P. Escudero*

The channel of Havana's port, where a few boats are anchored, is protected by the Castillo de los Tres Reyes del Morro.
- *Pierre Loubier*

As in all major cities, art in Havana takes many shapes and forms, such as fabric-painting.
- *P. Escudero*

Le Prado is one of the most pleasant areas in town, and sitting on a bench there is a surefire way to make new friends!
- *Pierre Loubier*

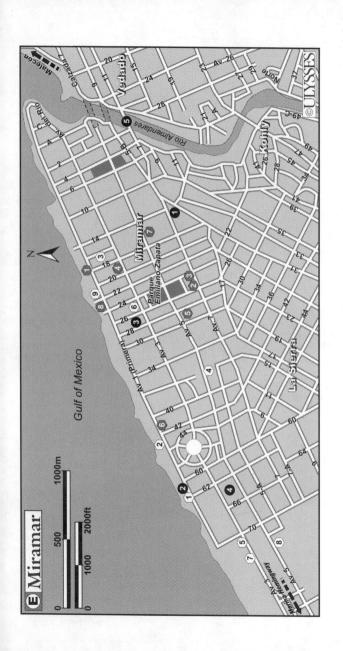

Miramar

Gulf of Mexico

Vedado

Miramar

Río Almendares

Kohly

La Sierra

Parque Emiliano Zapata

Av. 1ra (Primera)

Av. 3

Malecón

Calzada

Av. 26

Av. Norte

Marina Hemingway

© ULYSSES

or some of the finest restaurants in Havana.

Miramar is certainly not the most interesting part of the town, but there are some lovely homes to admire, especially on Avenida 5. Several of these houses have been turned into *tienda*-restaurants.

Russian Embassy

The best known is undoubtedly **La Maison** (*10am to 1pm; Calle 18, between Avenida 7 and Linea*), which was built in 1946 and made famous by its fashion shows, one of which Fidel's daughter participated in. Every evening at 10:15pm there is a fashion show and a music and dance show, for which there is an entrance fee of $10.

The **Acuario Nacional de Cuba** ★★ (*$7; Tue to Sun 10am to 6pm; Calle 60, at the corner of Avenida 1; ☎23-6401*) is a modern, well-maintained aquarium that presents exhibitions and dolphin and seal shows. The entrance is on Avenida 3.

The **Maqueta de La Habana** (*$3; Tue to Sat 9:30am to 5:30pm; Calle 28, between Avenida 1 and Avenida 3*) is impressive in itself, but since there is a model of the old city in Habana Vieja, its importance has diminished somewhat.

The **Russian Embassy** is worth a glance. It would actually be difficult not to see it, because it dominates Miramar like an enormous modern-day castle-fortress. It occupies a whole block of houses bordered by Calle 62 and Calle 66, between avenidas 3 and 5.

At the corner of Avenida 5 and Calle 26, in Miramar, there is a very beautiful park, the **Parque Emiliano Zapata**, named after the famous Mexican revolutionary.

Dotted with little fishing boats, the **Río Almendares** is truly picturesque. Its shores are liveliest around the **Puente de Hierro**. Cars are not allowed on this little steel drawbridge, which is used by thousands of cyclists to cross the Almandares. Vendors walk around selling meals, cakes and all sorts of items. There are a few small cafeterias in front of the Chinese restaurant El Mandarín (see p 168), on the Miramar side.

Tour F: The Hemingway Tour

A revolutionary by nature, the celebrated American writer and journalist Ernest Hemingway never tired of this city, where he began vacationing in the 1930s and then set up residence in 1939. Hemingway left an indelible stamp on Havana, and many local bars, restaurants and hotels claim him as a former patron. Following in his footsteps requires a stop at **La Bodeguita del Medio** (see p 164) for a *mojito*, a cocktail made of rum, lime juice, sugar and freshly crushed mint leaves. Next, head over to **La Floridita** (see p 165) for a second drink, but this time make it a daiquiri, the house specialty, supposedly invented right on the premises. The *papa especial* is Hemingway's personal mix, made with a double shot of three-year-old rum, lemon and crushed ice. Ask for the menu; this is one of the best restaurants in town! At the end of the evening, take a walk into the heart of Havana, to the **Hostal Valencia**, and ask for room no. 21, Hemingway's favourite. Here you can collapse on the bed and sleep off your cocktails, just like Hemingway used to do!

Die-hard Hemingway fans will want to head out to the Nobel Prize winner's sumptuous former residence, the **Finca la Vigía**, located about 15km (9.3mi) from town. Built in 1887, it is now the **Museo Ernest Hemingway ★★** *($2; Mon and Wed to Sat 9am to 4:30pm, Sun 9am to 1pm, closed on rainy days; San Francisco de Paula, ☎91-0809)*, though little has been altered since the author died in the United States. It contains many tastefully furnished, rustic rooms, a library with over 9,000 volumes, including original editions of a few of his novels and an assortment of his hunting trophies. Hemingway purchased this immense villa in 1940 after renting it for several months. Unfortunately, you can't actually go inside the house. However, the doors and windows are left wide open, so that visitors can peek in at the bar and look at various photographs, and retrace the life of one of America's most famous storytellers. A guided tour is essential to hear all sorts of anecdotes about Hemingway's fourth

Exploring

wife, Mary Welch, who lived here with him and had a tower built where he could write (he never used it though; his typewriter is on a high table on the ground floor; a leg wound forced him to work standing up). The Hemingways had 57 cats, which are buried in their own cemetery on the grounds. The animals lived on the second floor of the tower, which commands a panoramic view of the San Francisco de Paula valleys and of Havana, outlined in the distance.

Right near the big swimming pool (no swimming permitted), you'll find *El Pilar*, Hemingway's fishing boat, made famous by his numerous fishing chronicles and the novel *The Old Man and the Sea*. Surrounded by luxuriant tropical vegetation made up of no fewer than 18 different species, Hemingway's home is perched on a magnificent hill in the suburb of **San Francisco de Paula**, 10km (6.2mi) outside of Havana.

No Hemingway tour would be complete without a stop at the little port of **Cojimar ★**, where the famous author usually moored the *El Pilar*. Cojimar is located in the eastern beach area, about 10km (6.2mi) from Havana. It is easily accessible by car via the tunnel under the Bahía de La Habana; then follow the signs right after the stadium built for the Pan-American Games, which will be on your left. It is worth visiting Cojimar, if only to stroll along its winding streets. There are pretty little houses all along the coast. The village fishers erected a monument to Hemingway on the Malecón, in front of a small fortified tower. Follow the promenade to the excellent seafood restaurant **Las Terrazas**, one of Hemingway's favourite places to eat – a fact underscored by the many photographs on the walls (see p 173) . A few show Hemingway awarding Fidel Castro first prize in a fishing tournament.

Unlike other places in Havana with connections to Hemingway, at Las Terrazas you will find someone who actually knew him. Gregorio Fuentes, the hero of *The Old Man and the Sea* and captain of *El Pilar*, is almost part of the furniture at this restaurant. He has been eating lunch and dinner here like clockwork for years. Although he is 98 years old, if you're lucky (and understand Spanish), he just might tell you a few anecdotes about Hemingway and in so doing will take the opportunity to denounce the American embargo. During our visit to Las Terrazas, Gregorio Fuentes wasn't there, but we did get to enjoy a succulent seafood paella while gazing out at the bay. After our meal, we walked past the old man's modest home *(Calle Pesuela no. 209, between Buena Vista and Carmen)* and found him sitting on a chair in the street. Gregorio has a face that is reminiscent of the sea bed, a gritty complexion, pearly eyes and tousled hair. "Hemingway was a great man, a generous man with a big heart," he said to us by way of introduction. "In Cuba, Hemingway was happy." To flatter him, we told him jokingly that Hemingway might never have won the Nobel Prize for Literature without him, since he was the inspiration behind the novel *The Old Man and the Sea*. "He was a great writer, and I was just a skipper. *The Old Man and the Sea* is a true story."

The **Marina Hemingway**, near Miramar, is a sailing harbour presently undergoing massive development to cater to the needs of tourists. There is already an assortment of shops and restaurants, and several hotels are being built. This is a good place to get away from the hubbub of the city; you can stroll along canals stretching nearly 15km (9.3mi), rent a small

sailboat or a catamaran or relax on a pleasant terrace.

Tour G: The Southern Parks

La Habana is the smallest province in Cuba in terms of area, but it is also the most densely populated. As a result, it has no vast expanses of undeveloped land.

La Habana does, however, have two parks where you can enjoy some recreational activities. **Parque Lenin** *($2; Tue to Sun 10am to 6pm; Calle 100 and Cortina de la Presa)*, located 25km (15.5mi) outside the city, is a gigantic leisure centre. Built in 1972, it covers 750ha (1,878 acres) and includes a riding club, an amusement park, a sports complex, art galleries and an aquarium. Nothing has been left out at this giant playground, which used to be very popular with local residents. While you're in the area, you might want to stop for a meal at one of the province's finest restaurants, **Las Ruinas**.

The nearby **Jardín Botanico ★★** *($3; every day 8am to 4:30pm; Km 3.5 of the Carretera del Rosario)*, also about 25km (15.5mi) from the city, is sure to be a hit with plant-lovers and those

Exploring

who enjoy wide-open spaces. Covering an area of 600ha (1,482 acres), the numerous gardens are linked by 35km (21.7mi) of roads and are so vast that you'll want to use your car or climb aboard the little tractor-pulled train. The gardens contain a large collection of tropical and subtropical plants from all five continents. The Jardín Botanico is divided into three large sections, one for the various plant species and soils of Cuba, another for tropical and subtropical vegetation from Central America, the Antilles, Asia and the South Pacific and finally a series of greenhouses in three pavilions. The meticulously reproduced Japanese garden is one of the loveliest, graced with fountains and a waterfall, in front of which stands the Restaurante Ecológico (see p 173). Another restaurant, the Restaurante El Ranchón (see p 173), lies hidden in a forest of pine trees. A large research centre and the botany department of the Universidad de La Habana are also located on the grounds of the Jardín Botanico.

Tour H: The Eastern Beaches

There are some excellent beaches just a few kilometres from Havana. The most inviting one is definitely the **Santa Maria Beach ★**, an expanse of white sand that is every bit as lovely as the beaches of Varadero. The village itself is devoted essentially to tourism, and has many hotels. Also very beautiful, the beaches of **Boca Ciega ★**, the neighbouring village to the east, are overlooked by many tourists. Boca Ciega is a charming village of small vacation homes owned by *Habaneros*. Farther east is the village of **Guanabo ★**, which doesn't have the most attractive beaches in the area, but offers the widest range of waterfront activities. If you are staying in Havana, these beaches are worth a daytrip; in fact, they are so close that you can even come here for half a day.

The roads linking the various beaches are in excellent condition and are generally fairly well marked. The simplest route is to take the road that leads from Habana Vieja through the Bahía de La Habana tunnel and then past the stadium built for the Pan-American Games. If you go this way, you'll be on the white sandy beaches of Santa Maria in less than 20min.

You can also take a quieter and more picturesque road that runs past a number of villages and farmer's fields. To do so, take Avenida Máximo Gomez to Via Blanca. If you are only staying in Cuba for a week, this is the perfect chance to venture inland. This route takes half an hour to an hour longer than the one mentioned above, due to the traffic on the little country road.

Accommodations

In Havana, you can either stay in a hotel or a *casa particular*, a room rented in a private home.

In general, hotels are of high quality here and offer all the necessary conveniences. Some hotels have more charm than others, regardless of whether they are in Old Havana, Centro or the Vedado, but most offer the same comfort. The majority of hotels have their own restaurants.

Casas particulares are something else. There is no better way to experience the Cuban way of life, but here the difference between one place and another can be enormous. Prices vary from $15 to $25. Take note, however, if someone takes you to one of these houses, that person receives a commission of $5 for each day of your stay. This surplus may be slipped onto your bill, which otherwise can be negotiated. Go and visit a few rooms before making a choice. Some have all the

conveniences while others may not even have a fan. Because these *casas particulares* usually have only one or two rooms, we do not provide precise addresses but we do indicate areas where they are concentrated. To find out which houses rent rooms, look for small, well-placed notices that say *Aqui se alquila habitacion a extranjeros*.

Tour A: The Old City

See map p 79

The hotel business is booming in the old city. Small historic residences dating from colonial times are increasingly being integrated into the hotel system. Each of these residences would be worth mentioning in the chapter on "Exploring." They are all charming and often more luxurious than you would expect, and all this in the heart of one of the world's best-preserved colonial cities.

Residencia Académica del Convento de Santa Clara
$25
⊗, *pb, tv*
Calle Cuba no. 610, between Calle Luz and Calle Sol
☎*61-3335*
≈*33-5696*
One place with a great deal of colonial atmosphere is certainly the Residencia Académica del Convento de Santa Clara. This convent, built during the first half of the 17th century, remains incredibly charming. Situated a little off the tourist track, it has a peacefulness

that is sometimes missing in other parts of Old Havana. Because this establishment only has a few guest rooms and academics passing through have priority, it is better to telephone first or to reserve in advance.

Hostal Valencia
$46-$60
≡, ℜ, *pb*, ⊗
Calle Oficios no. 53
☎*62-3801*
≈*33-5628*
The Hostal Valencia lies 200m (656ft) from the Plaza de Armas, in one of the loveliest sections of Old Havana. This small, 12-room hotel is extremely charming and authentic, and is sure to appeal to visitors with a romantic bent. Nowhere else is *el sabor cubano* more tangible! This 18th-century palace is built around an inner court, a pleasant place to relax, read, get your bearings or simply to meet some Cubans. The rooms are rustic and very clean, and the service is extremely friendly. The place is very popular, though, so try to reserve a room as far in advance as possible. Some rooms do not have air conditioning. If you're lucky, you might land in room no. 21, where Ernest Hemingway used to stay when he came to Havana. The breakfasts served in the restaurant La Paella are very generous, and at dinnertime

you won't regret abandoning Cuban cuisine for the night and sampling an authentic Valencian *paella*.

Ambos Mundos
$65-$90
≡, *pb*, ☎, *tv*, ℜ
Calle Obispo no. 153
at Mercedes
☎*66-9529*
⇌*60-9532*
Made famous by Ernest Hemingway, who lived here in the 1930s, when this part of the city was an artistic and intellectual centre, the Ambos Mundos is a luxury hotel located a stone's throw from the many cafés frequented by the eminent writer. You can even visit his old room, no. 511, which has been kept intact. The view of Old Havana from the hotel's top floors is magnificent. The turn-of-the-century ambiance is still palpable in of the vintage Otis elevator and the lobby made entirely of wood, in the middle of which stands an equally old grand piano.

Hotel Conde de Villanueva
$67-$95
≡, ℝ, ℜ, *pb*, *tv*, ☎
Calle Mercaderes no. 202, corner Calle Lamparilla
☎*62-9293*
⇌*62-9682*
Hotel Conde de Villanueva has nine very beautiful, but somewhat dark, rooms. Other hotels in the area may have more attractive

patios but this place is pleasant and is right next to Plaza Vieja. Built in 1724, the hotel is named after its most renowned former owner, Claudio Martínez de Pinillo, conte de Villanueva, who was city treasurer from 1825 to 1851.

🛶 **Hotel Florida**
$75-$105
≡, ℜ, *pb*, *tv*
Calle Obispo no. 252, corner Calle Cuba
☎*62-4127*
⇌*62-4117*
Hotel Florida is situated in a magnificent colonial residence dating from the 1830s. Converted into a hotel with its present name in 1875, this dwelling was transformed into a *casa de vivienda (solar)* after the Revolution. It was also used as a tourist information centre for a short period before reverting to a hotel in 1999. The hotel has 25 rooms on three floors. Although a bit sombre, they are pleasant enough and are set out around a splendid patio. It is a wonderful place with undeniable charm.

Hostal El Comendador
$80-$110
≡, ℜ, *pb*, *tv*
Calle Justiz, corner Calle Officios
☎*62-3801*
⇌*33-5628*
Hostal El Comendador is under the same administration as Hotel Valencia. It is

Titles for Sale

The Santa Isabel hotel is situated in the former palace of Nicolás Martínes de Campos, who became Conde de Santovenia in 1824. In fact, titles could easily be bought in colonial Cuba. The title of marquis cost about $45,000 whereas one could become a count for $25,000 to $30,000, payable to the Spanish Crown. Many rich plantation owners made themselves nobles this way. During the 1840s, Cuba had 34 marquis and 32 counts, most of whom resided in Havana.

a good example of the intelligent way Old Havana is being developed, with respect for its history and architecture. Even though the two hotels are connected, they are treated as two distinct entities in order to preserve their historic character. The Comendador's 14 rooms are small but luxurious. They are also situated around a patio, which gives the place its colonial look. Interestingly, major archaeological excavations are taking place beneath the foundations of the house. Vestiges from the beginning of the colony of San Cristóbal de La Habana have been found, and a small room has been set up so visitors can follow the progress of the archaeological dig. To rent a room here, you must go to Hotel Valencia; the entrance is on Calle Officios, at the corner of Calle Justiz.

Hostal del Tejadillo
Prices not available
approx. $80-$100
≡, ℝ, ℜ, K, ☎, pb, tv
Calle Tejadillo no. 12, corner Calle San Ignacio
☎ 63-7283
≈ 63-8830

The opening of Hostal del Tejadillo is scheduled for summer 2000, so it is worth mentioning. The 32-room hotel is made up of three separate but connecting houses from the 18th and 19th centuries. Situated next to Plaza de la Catedral, it should be one of the most enjoyable places in Old Havana.

🏨 Santa Isabel
$110-$150
≡, pb, ☎, tv, ℜ
Calle Baratoillo no. 9
at Calle Obispo
☎33-8201
≈33-8391

Caressed by the gentle breeze from the Bahia de La Habana, the colonial building of the Santa Isabel is sure to give you the impression that you stepped back more than a century in time. Leading out onto the Plaza de Armas where second-hand booksellers peddle their revolutionary literature, it is undeniably charming. Enormous doors link the various rooms, decorated in colonial Cuban style and offering flawless comfort. As a matter of fact, the pope stayed here during his famous January 1998 visit, just steps from the cathedral.

Tour B: The Prado and Parque Central

See map p 107

The hotels around the Prado and Parque Central are usually larger and more modern that those in the old city. Their style is definitely neo-classical and the atmosphere livelier and more cheerful. Staying here, one feels like a traveller from the end of the 19th century happily discovering an alternative, civilized city. The hotel sector here is developing as rapidly as in the old colonial city, but the size of the projects makes the process longer and more costly. The restoration of Hotel Telegrafo, at the corner of Prado and Calle Neptuno, is the best example of this trend.

Hotel Lido
$18-$25
ℜ, pb, ⊗, cold water only
Calle Consulado no. 210
☎62-0653

The Hotel Lido, with its pleasant terrace that stays open late into the night, attracts independent travellers. The service is extremely friendly. Although this place is not unappealing, it has no air conditioning, which can make for long nights when the weather is hot. Those who prefer sleeping with the window open won't have any problem, however, as most of the rooms open onto balconies overlooking a quiet street.

Casa del Cientifico
$25-$31 sb, ⊗
$45-$55 pb, ≡
≡, ℜ, pb, ☎, ctv
Prado 212, at the corner of Trocadero
☎62-4511 or 63-8103
≈63-8103

La Casa del Cientifico is in another old colonial building in the very heart of Havana. It welcomes passing scientists, but others can

Accommodations

find accommodation here now and again, when the place has vacancies. The establishment offers the best quality for the price. Indeed, you will have the impression of staying in a 19th-century mansion – especially since the nation's president lived here at the turn of the century. With its neoclassical interior courtyard and balcony overlooking the Prado, this hotel is worth the detour.

Hotel Caribbean
$30-$48
≡, ℜ, pb, cold water only
Avenida Paseo del Prado no. 164
☎60-8233

Very popular with visitors on a shoestring budget, the Hotel Caribbean has a friendly atmosphere. Its excellent location, right on the Paseo del Prado, is its main attraction. It lies within walking distance of the old city, the Malecón and even the Vedado. There are a number of inexpensive restaurants in the area as well. The place is a little outdated, but clean; the watchword here is simplicity. A few of the rooms have air conditioning, making them a real bargain for the price. Last but not least, guests are allowed to use the swimming pool at the Hotel Sevilla.

Hotel Inglaterra
$75-$100
≡, ℜ, pb, ctv
Avenida Paseo del Prado no. 416
☎33-8593
≈33-8254

Located in front of Parque Central and right near the Capitolio, the Hotel Inglaterra is very popular with travellers of all kinds. Local artists and intellectuals used to gather here once upon a time. This hotel, built in 1875, has a distinctive character and looks slightly outdated, but still reflects the splendour of the turn of the century. It is the oldest hotel in Cuba, and its architecture and historical importance have earned it official status as a national monument. The decor is perfectly suited to the majestic neoclassical facade. The relaxing bar/restaurant at the entrance is patronized by travellers with an adventurous air about them – a fairly colourful crowd on the whole. The rooftop bar offers one of the best views in town. The rooms, soberly decorated with antique furniture, are very beautiful. Keep in mind that those with a balcony face onto Parque Central, a noisy area with a lot of traffic.

Hotel Plaza
$80-$120
≡, ℜ, pb, ctv
Calle Ignacio Agramonte no. 167
at the corner of Calle Neptuno
☎33-8583 to 90 or 57-1075
⇆33-8591

Near Parque Central, the
Hotel Plaza has a unique
charm about it. Its fountains
and high-ceilinged entrance
create a wonderful ambi-
ance. The rooms are clean
and all have air conditioning (which can, however,
be a bit loud).

Hotel Sevilla
$100-$130
≡, ≈, ℜ, pb, ctv
Calle Trocadero no. 55
☎60-8560
⇆60-8582

The architecture and decor
of the Hotel Sevilla's lobby
will transport you to
Andalusia. This lovely turn-
of-the-century hotel has
been entirely renovated,
and the mood here falls
somewhere between re-
laxed elegance and a cer-
tain Mediterranean offhand-
edness. Located between
the Paseo del Prado and the
Museo de la Revolución, the
Sevilla is just a few
steps from the old city.
Come nightfall, however,
the streets around the hotel
are rather dark and empty.
If you plan on walking
about at night, you're better
off staying at the Inglaterra
or the Plaza in this part of
Havana. The Sevilla's rooms
are a bit outmoded for the

price, and the wall-cover-
ings and furnishings show
signs of wear in places.
Nevertheless, if you can
afford this place, you'll certainly be enchanted. The
Sevilla's clientele consists
mainly of European tourists.
It has three restaurants, and
offers a package rate that
includes morning and eve-
ning meals. The buffet-style
breakfast served on the
ground floor features a
well-balanced assortment of
fruit, meat and pastries. The
fresh rolls, occasionally
topped with pineapple, are
among the best in Havana.
In the shopping arcade on
the lower floor is a restaurant that serves traditional
Andalusian cuisine; the
Roof Garden on the ninth
floor is one of the finest
and most beautiful restaurants in the capital.

Hotel Parque Central
$128-$165
≡, ℜ, pb, ☎, ctv, ≈
Neptuno, between the Prado and
Zulueta
☎66-6627 to 29
⇆60-6630

The Hotel Parque Central is
the newest addition to the
capital's central district. The
hotel offers exquisite luxury. Not only does it boast
impeccably comfortable
rooms, a rooftop pool and a
conference room, but it is
also remarkably well situated, near the park, the
Capitolio and Habana Vieja.

Accommodations

Hotel Lincoln and the Revolutionary Struggle

Hotel Lincoln located in the Centro, conceals an interesting story behind its facade. In fact, on February 23, 1958, the day before the Gran Premio car race that was then held annually in Havana, the world-champion racing-car driver, Juan Manuel Fangio was kidnapped by a commando of the Movimiento 26 de Julio led by Oscar Lucero. The Argentinean, five times world champion between 1951 and 1957, was forced to follow his abductors at gunpoint. He was taken to a residence in the suburbs of the Vedado where he was kept under surveillance for two days before being let go. Apparently, he was delighted by his experience.

This striking feat made the front page in the international press. The Cuban crisis was given daily media coverage, and, the rebels' cause attracted sympathy around the world. The kidnapping of Fangio was a turning point in the revolutionary force's fight against the Batista regime. A plaque embedded in the wall outside the hotel commemorates this important event.

Tour C: The Centro

See map p 115

For *casas particulares*, the best thing to do is to look in the streets west of the Prado. Consulado, Industria, Crespo and all the streets that intersect them between the Malecón and Virtudes are fertile hunting ground. Do not hesitate to visit a few until you find one that pleases you. As already mentioned, the quality varies greatly from one place to another. You can always negotiate a bit and find one for a good price.

Hotel New York
$15
sb, ®
Calle Dragones 156
☎*62-5260*

Hotel New York, a large building in the middle of downtown, is mainly frequented by Cubans passing through the capital. The decor is modest and the noise may disturb some guests. The rooms themselves could not be simpler, but at least each one of them has a fan. Moreover, the price is unbeatable. You may be refused access under the pretext that the hotel is reserved exclusively for Cubans. Bargain hunters will thus have the opportunity to test their powers of persuasion.

Hotel Isla de Cuba
$18
≡, *pb*
Calle Monte no. 169, between Calle Cienfuegos and Calle Aponte
☎*62-1031*

The Hotel Isla de Cuba is under renovation. Nobody seems to know exactly when it will reopen but the price of its rooms should remain about the same. This factor, in addition to its very practical location opposite Parque de la Fraternidad, makes it a place worth noting.

Hotel Lincoln
$28-$37, bkfst incl.
≡, ℜ, *pb, tv*
Calle Galiano between Calle Virtudes and Calle Anima
☎*33-8209*

The Hotel Lincoln, at the edge of the old city, has an essentially Cuban clientele. It is a bit old-fashioned, but its rooftop bar/restaurant affords a unique view of the city.

Hotel Deauville
$42-$54
≡, ℜ, *pb, tv*
Calle Galiano, at the corner of the Malecón
☎*62-8051 to 59*

The Hotel Deauville is centrally located right on the Malecón, not far from the old city. The place is a little noisy, so it's best to request a room on the upper floors facing the sea.

Tour D: The Vedado

See map p 121

The Vedado has rooms in modern buildings without much colonial flavour. However, for people who don't want to be too disoriented and prefer being in the business district, it's not a bad idea to stay here.

Accommodations

The best place to look for *casas particulares* is near the main entrance to the university, on the streets bordering Calle San Lázaro and especially to the west above Calle Infanta. The residents here are used to dealing with strangers. Again, the quality of the rooms varies greatly. Visit a few of them before renting one.

Hotel Universitario
$25-$34
≡, ℜ, pb, ☎, ctv
Calle 17, corner Calle K and Calle L, opposite the gas station
The very hospitable Hotel Universitario is perfectly located to avoid the expense of taking taxis, but is also in pleasant surroundings. The lobby's elegant and well-arranged furniture equals the comfort of the rooms.

Colina
$50 bkfst incl.
≡, ℜ, pb, ☎, ctv
Calle L between Calles 27 and Jovelar
☎33-4103
⇆33-4104
Right next to the university, the Colina is not very inviting. Indeed, the hotel lacks light, plants and that certain something that gives a place appeal. Fans of Cuban literature, however, will want to attend literary events held here at night.

Hotel Capri
$65-$80, bkfst incl.
≡, ≈, ℜ, pb, ctv
Calle 21, at the corner of Calle N
☎33-3747
⇆33-3750
The Hotel Capri is a good deal. A legacy of the American mafia, it has an attractive lobby, and the pool, located on the roof of the tall building, offers an extraordinary panoramic view. The restaurants, unfortunately, are in the basement.

Hotel St. John's
$65-$80
≡, ℜ, pb, tv
Calle O no. 206, between Calle 23 and Calle 25
☎33-3740
⇆33-3561
The Hotel St.John's, located in the heart of the Vedado commercial area, near La Rampa, is a real bargain for the money. The service is pleasant, the atmosphere is relaxed and the rooms are well kept. Many visiting Latin Americans stay here.

Hotel Vedado
$65-$80
≡, ℜ, pb, tv
Calle O no. 244, between La Rampa and Calle 25
☎33-4072
⇆33-4186
Hotel Vedado is low on charm, but it is decent and well located.

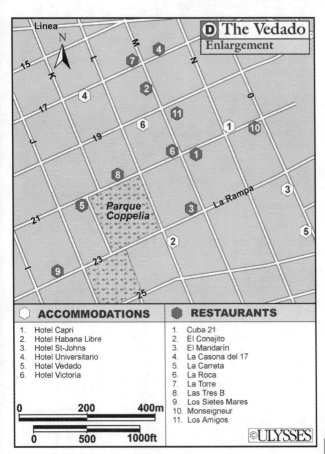

ACCOMMODATIONS

1. Hotel Capri
2. Hotel Habana Libre
3. Hotel St-Johns
4. Hotel Universitario
5. Hotel Vedado
6. Hotel Victoria

RESTAURANTS

1. Cuba 21
2. El Conejito
3. El Mandarín
4. La Casona del 17
5. La Carreta
6. La Roca
7. La Torre
8. Las Tres B
9. Los Sietes Mares
10. Monseigneur
11. Los Amigos

0   200   400m

0   500   1000ft

©ULYSSES

Accommodations

Hotel Habana Libre
$80-$120
≡, ≈, ℝ, ℜ, pb, ctv
Calle L, at the corner of Calle 23
☎33-4011
⇌33-3141

The immense Hotel Habana Libre, formerly the Hilton, looks like a bit like a factory. The ambiance, however, is unparalleled. The Habana Libre lies at the centre of La Rampa, and is surrounded by all sorts of little shops.

Hotel Victoria
$80-$100
≡, ℝ, ℜ, pb, ctv
Calle 19, at the corner of Calle M
☎33-3510
⇌33-3109
reserva@victo.gca.cma.net

The Hotel Victoria caters to travelling businesspeople and vaunts itself as the chicest five-star hotel in Havana. Combining luxury and tradition, it offers personalized service and an elegant ambiance. This small hotel also has a pool at the back.

Habana Riviera
$85-$120
≡, ℜ, pb, ☎, ctv
Calle Paseo, at the Malecón
☎33-4051
⇌33-3739

Habana Riviera is pleasantly situated by the sea. This former Mafioso haunt gives you a taste of Cuba in the 1950s, before the Miramar region became a tourist mecca. It is characterized by old-fashioned luxury and somewhat bizarre taste that can even be called kitsch. As for the rest, the hotel is very comfortable and offers most services.

Hotel Presidente
$90-$140
≡, ℜ, pb, tv
Calle Calzada no. 110, corner Avenida G
☎33-4394
⇌33-3753

Situated in a magnificent neoclassical building constructed in 1928, this hotel is quite attractive and its location, on Avenida de los Presidentes right next to the Malecón, is perfect. The rooms are not very large but they are pleasant and tastefully decorated. The place is quiet and definitely worth considering.

Hotel Nacional
$120-$170, bkfst incl.
≡, ≈, ℝ, ℜ, pb, ctv
Calle O, at the corner of Calle 21
☎33-3564
⇌33-5054

The Hotel Nacional is without question the most beautiful hotel in Havana, and is remarkably charming for a place of its size. Its five stars are well deserved. The entrance, built in 1930, the vast gardens and the magnificent swimming pool will soon make you forget you're in the middle of the city. The rooms have ultramodern furnishings; those with a view of the sea are especially desirable. Visitors

The Battle of Hotel Nacional

While contemplating the Hotel Nacional's quiet charm, it is hard to imagine that the place could have been the scene of a battle on October 2, 1933. And yet the officers of regular army, who had played a part in the "Revolt of the Sargents," had been entrenched on these premises since the first days of September. This was the site of one of the most violent confrontations of the 1933 revolution, which overthrew the dictator Machado.

Nearly 300 officers at the centre of a counter-revolutionary movement, were barricaded in the hotel in order to avoid confronting the insurrec-

tionary forces. Batista, who had recently become head of the army, had hoped to force their surrender by cutting the Nacional's water and electricity, but seeing that this did not weaken the determination of its occupants, he called for an attack at 6am on October 2. First with light infantry and then with heavy artillery, the hotel was bombarded on all sides, even from the sea by the Cuban navy's cruiser *Cuba*. It was only at 4:45pm that the officers surrendered. Many were killed there and the hotel was subjected to a systematic pillage by army rabble.

looking for a good restaurant to enhance their stay will be thrilled by the buffet. The ambiance is particularly interesting, with journalists, film directors and

businesspeople rubbing shoulders in the gardens and the lobby. It also hosts the prestigious Latin American Film Festival in December.

Accommodations

Hotel Melia Cohiba
$165-$215
≡, ≈, ℝ, ℜ, *pb*, *ctv*
Calle Paseo, at the corner of Calle 1
☎*33-3636*
⇄*33-4555*

The brand new Hotel Melia Cohiba is the most modern five-star hotel in Cuba. A symbol of the phenomenal expansion of the tourist industry, it is not the place to go if you're looking for authentic Cuban charm.

Plaza de la Revolución

Hotel Bruzón
$17-$23
≡, *sb*, ⊗
Calle Bruzón no. 217, between Av. Rancho Boyeros and Calle Pozos Dulces
☎*57-5684*

This is the only hotel in this area of the city. It's adequate if you have to take an early morning bus – the Terminal de Ómnibus Interprovinciales is on the next street – otherwise, it isn't very interesting. Far from everything and in a bland neighbourhood, the place has a danceclub that makes it noisy as well.

Tour E: Miramar

See map p 129

This region has been experiencing a hotel boom over the last few years. Hotel complexes are being built

farther and farther west along the coast. The hotels in Miramar are generally quieter than those in the Vedado and the old city. On the other hand, it takes money and time to get to the most interesting places in the city.

The Residencia Universitaria Ispaje
$35-$40 FAP
≡, *pb*, ☎, *ctv*, ≈
Avenidas 1 and 22
☎*23-5370 or 23-6633*

The Residencia Universitaria Ispaje is located by the sea, before the large hotel complexes. This small 12-room hotel mainly welcomes university professors, but anyone else can stay here provided there are vacancies. The rooms are clean and well-appointed, and the outdoor swimming pools, when they are actually filled with water, are a pleasure.

Hostal Icemar
$27-$39
≡, *pb*, ☎, *ctv*
104 Calle 16, between Avenidas 1 and 3
☎*23-6130*

Just outside the hotel zone, Hostal Icemar has an ambiance that is much less stuffy than that of Miramar's huge complexes. The rooms are simple and comfortable and there is a terrace in the interior courtyard adjacent to a small cafeteria. Also close to the sea.

Hotel Villamar
$29
≡, *pb*, *tv*
Avenida 3 no. 2402, corner Calle 24
☎*33-3778*
Situated in a strange house
that is reminiscent of a me-
dieval castle, this small hotel looks bizarre and out of
place. Its eight rooms are
modest but decent and are
all arranged around a little
terrace overlooking
Avenida 3.

🦐 Hotel Mirazul
$45-$60
≡, ℝ, ℜ, *tv*
Avenida 5 no. 3603,
between Calle 36 and Calle 40
☎*33-0088*
⇄*33-0045*
Pleasant and welcoming,
this small hotel has eight
large, charming rooms. The
atmosphere complements
the bourgeois style of the
house, which was built at
the end of the 1940s.

Bosque Gaviota
$58 bkfst incl.
≡, ℜ, *pb*, ☎, *ctv*, ≈
Avenida 28A, between Calles 49A and
49C
☎*24-9232*
⇄*24-5637*
The Bosque
Gaviota is
also set back
from the
coast. The
expanse
that
stretches

beyond the outdoor terrace
leads to a river. The palce is
breathtaking. The hotel,
which opened in 1998, has
undeniable charm and de-
lightful rooms. Request a
room with a view of the
backyard overflowing with
greenery. The Gaviota's
restaurant offers nightly
salsa shows.

Novotel Miramar
$100-$130
≡, *pb*, ℝ, ℜ, =, ☎, *tv*
Avenida 5, between Calle 72
and Calle 76
☎*24-3584*
⇄*24-3583*
Novotel Miramar is an ultra-
chic hotel complex of the
sort that are springing up all
over Miramar. This is a
modern, attractive hotel
with neo-Renaissance style
murals, which make it surprisingly inviting. The
rooms are painted in relaxing tones of blue and yellow and provide ev-
ery comfort. Unfortu-
nately, the views
from the hotel are
rather unpleasant:
one has the impres-
sion of being in
the middle of
huge vacant lot in
which a few bits
of construction
make vain attempts to
be pleasing.

Accommodations

Hotel Kohly
$55-$62
≡, ℜ, pb, ☎, tv, =
Calle 49, corner Avenida 36A
Kohly
☎*24-0240*
⇋*24-1733*
Hotel Kohly is somewhat far from everything but it is modern and fairly attractive.

Bellocaribe
$61-$77
≡, ℜ, pb, ☎, ctv
Calle158 at Calle 31
☎*33-9906 to 09*
⇋*33-6839*
The Bellocaribe is located next to the capital's biotechnology research centre, and thus mainly receives scientists. It offers no real advantage to passing tourists, however, save perhaps for its buffet-restaurant which serves one of the most commendable cuisines in the capital. A superb miniature jungle makes up part of the interior.

Hotel Neptuno
$70-$90
≡, ≈, ℜ, pb, ctv
Avenida 3, at the corner of Calle 70
☎*24-1606*
⇋*24-0042*
The Hotel Neptuno, located in one of the two big towers near the imposing Russian embassy, is decidedly lacking in charm. It is almost entirely made of concrete, the orange upholstered furniture is outdated, and the big dining room

looks more like a school cafeteria than a restaurant. On the other hand, the balconies of some of the rooms offer panoramic views of the sea, and the swimming pool, flanked by gardens, is extremely attractive. The other tower houses the **Triton** hotel, managed by the same chain and virtually identical to its twin. Indeed, there is no difference between the two as far as comfort and quality are concerned.

Hotel Copacabana
$83-$126 bkfst incl.
≡, ≈, ℜ, pb, ctv
Avenida 1, at the corner of Calle 44
☎*24-1037*
⇋*24-2846*
The Hotel Copacabana has a pretty friendly, relaxed atmosphere for such a big place. All the rooms offer a partial view of the sea. The hotel nightclub is packed almost every night.

Palco

$94

≡, ℜ, pb, ☎, ctv

Calle 146 between Avenidas 11 and 1

☎33-7235

⇋33-7236

Offering the same basic services as superior-grade hotels, the Palco is located near the convention centre. The luxury complex's 180 rooms are generally occupied by people attending conventions and seminars.

Chateau Miramar

$95-$120

≡, ℜ, pb, ☎, ⇋, ctv, ≈

Avenida 1, between Calles 60 and 62

☎24-1952

⇋24-0224

reservas@chateau.cha.cyt.cu

One of Miramar's newest luxury hotels, the Chateau Miramar is fully equipped to receive businesspeople and the most demanding of clients. Since the hotel has only 50 rooms, it offers more personalized service.

El Viejo y El Mar

$150

≡, ≈, ℝ, ℜ, pb, ctv

Marina Hemingway

☎24-6336

⇋24-6823

El Viejo y El Mar, named after Ernest Hemingway's famous novel (*The Old Man and the Sea*), is located at the Marina Hemingway. It has been completely renovated and is run by Delta, a Canadian hotel chain. This place is far from the hub-

bub of the city and has a swimming pool and a gym.

Melia-Habana

$175-$215

≡, ℜ, pb, ☎, ctv, ≈

Avenida 3, between Calles 76 and 80

☎24-8500

⇋24-8505

depres@habana.solmelia.cma.net

The Melia-Habana is Miramar's newest hotel. It offers the utmost in luxury, with all the perks imaginable. Indeed, rooms don't get more comfortable than this. The hotel looks out onto the sea, but the beach (like others in the Miramar region) is not well tended. The swimming pools here are more pleasant thanks to their enormous size and the many promenades surrounding them. The hotel is located halfway between the old city and the airport.

Tour H: The Eastern Beaches

The shoreline between Havana and Varadero is studded with hotels. There is something for every taste and budget. You can easily rent a bedroom or even an entire house in any of the little coastal villages along the way. This is definitely the cheapest option, and often one of the most pleasant. All you have to do is ask a Cuban in one of the local restaurants, hotels or

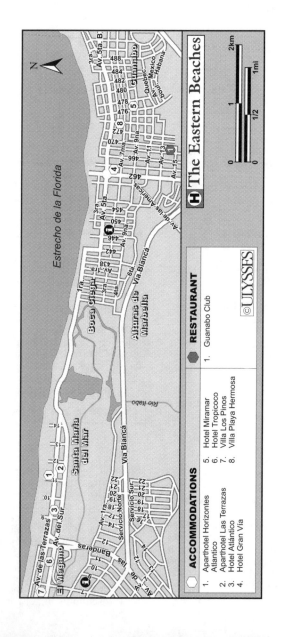

N

Estrecho de la Florida

Santa María del Mar

Río Itabo

Via Blanca

Alturas de Via Blanca
Marbella

Boca Ciega

Guanabo

H The Eastern Beaches

0   1/2   1   1mil

0   1   2km

ACCOMMODATIONS

1. Aparthotel Horizontes Atlántico
2. Aparthotel Las Terrazas
3. Hotel Atlántico
4. Hotel Gran Vía
5. Hotel Miramar
6. Hotel Tropicoco
7. Villa Los Pinos
8. Villa Playa Hermosa

RESTAURANT

1. Guanabo Club

© ULYSSES

shops if he or she happens to know of a safe, comfortable and friendly place to stay (*Conoce alguien que alquila cuartos?*), and you're set! Although this practice is very common, especially in this region, it is still technically illegal. For the cheapest hotels and rooms, go to Boca Ciega or Guanabo.

El Abra
$18 per cabin
ℜ, ≈, ⊗

About 65km (40mi) from Havana, along the road that leads past the Playas del Este to Varadero and the province of Matanzas, there are two campgrounds open year-round. Nestled between the sea and two hills, El Abra is a campground that also rents out modest little cabins. It has good facilities and its beach is superb, mainly because of its unspoiled natural setting. Introductory scuba courses are offered at the swimming pool, and packages for excursions from the Canimar marina are sold on the premises. El Abra is also the starting point for outings on the Río Canimar. The underwater scenery in front of the campground is superb, as are the trails in the surrounding mountains.

A few of the latter have been designed for nature lovers, making it easy to observe the local flora and fauna. The meals served in the restaurant are excellent, especially if you order à la carte. The house specialty is pork. If you decide to rent a *cabaña*, make sure it's clean first. Also, don't leave food there, as squirrels and rodents apparently go scavenging when nobody is home.

Villa Playa Hermosa
$22-$30
Avenida 7, between Calle 472 and Calle 474
☎96-2774

At the foot of the hill, right near the sea, the Villa Playa Hermosa is a series of small, fully equipped cottages. The place is unfortunately a bit noisy, since buses and trucks travel along nearby Avenida 5 during the day.

Hotel Gran Via
$25
≡, ℜ, pb, ☎, ctv
at Avenida 5 and Calle 462, Guanabo
☎96-2271

Hotel Gran Via is less luxurious than its neighbours, but has the same excellent level of comfort. The rooms are inviting, albeit tiny. The building also houses the coziest of restaurants and bars. Inexpensive accommodations right on the beach.

Aparthotel Horizontes Atlántico
$40-$60
≡, K, ℝ, ≈, ℜ , pb, tv
Avenida de las Terrazas no. 21, between Calle 11 and Calle 12, Santa María del Mar
☎97-1203
⇝97-1494

The white, sandy beach at the seaside resort of Santa Maria stretches several kilometres and is lined with hotels. The Aparthotel Horizontes Atlántico is the least expensive choice in this area. The rooms are decorated with simple furnishings and all have a balcony and a refrigerator. Some have a kitchen and a dining room as well. All you have to do is cross one street, and
 you're at the beach.

Hotel Tropicoco
$40-$60 FAP
≡, ≈, ℜ, pb, ctv
Avenida de las Terrazas
☎97-1371
⇝97-1389

The Hotel Tropicoco is hands-down one of the most popular hotel is Hotel Tropicoco, due to its all-inclusive packages, which include lodging, meals, drinks and non-motorized sports activities (cycling, windsurfing, catamaran sailing). The hotel has 188 rooms, some of which offer a view of the sea. Its night-

club is also very popular after dark.

Aparthotel Las Terrazas
$45
≡, K, ℝ, ℜ, pb, ☎, ctv, ≈
Avenida Las Terrazas, near Calle 10, Playa Santa Maria del Mar
☎97-1344
⇝97-1316

A stone's throw from the turquoise sea, the Aparthotel Las Terrazas offers fully equipped, simple and comfortable apartments. The beach is very pleasant, but often crowded on weekends. Though the interior of the buildings is particularly charming, the same cannot be said for the hospital-like exterior, whose light-green colour tries in vain to recall the sea. Better to go straight to the beach!

Hotel Miramar
$50
ℝ, ℜ, pb, tv, ⊗
Calle 9, between Calle 476 and Calle 478
☎96-2507 or 96-2262

The Hotel Miramar, in Guanabo, is perched on a hill overlooking the sea. This tranquil, inviting place is much less touristy than the hotels in Santa Maria. The rooms are small but pleasant, and some offer a view of the sea. Poolside festivities and barbecues are organized regularly, so if you're looking for peace and quiet, don't take a room facing the pool.

Panamericano Resort
$56-$68
≡, ℜ, pb, ☎, tv, ≈
at Calle A and Avenida Central
Cojimar
☎33-8545 or 33-8811
⇄33-8580

The Pananericano Resort is the first hotel in the eastern beaches region when coming from the capital, but it is nowhere near the beach! To compensate, the hotel offers its   guests a daily mini-bus service to Havana. Built to welcome dignitaries and other representatives of the 1991 Pan-American Games, the hotel is lacklustre in style and is already a bit worn. On the other hand, a bar, several restaurants, a pool and a nightclub make the place more appealing and compensate for the small rooms.

Marina Puerto Sol Tarará
$57-$79
≡, ✪, ℜ, pb, ☎, ctv, ≈
Via Blanca, Km 19, Tarará
☎97-1462
⇄97-4499

Prior to the Revolution, wealthy Americans would spend their holidays at the Marina Puerto Sol Tarará. Today the marina attracts travellers from other countries with its well-appointed cottages and many services, including a fitness centre

offering massage and acupuncture as well as introductory scuba-diving lessons. The beach is certainly one of the most pleasant, as it is more private and thus less frequented.

Hotel Megano
$57-$74
≡, ℜ, pb, ☎, ctv, ≈
Via Blanca, Km 22
☎97-1610
⇄97-1624

Hotel Megano is 500m (1,600ft) from the beach and seems only to cater to tourists going through certain agencies. During our visit, for instance, the great majority of guests were Italian. The place is luxurious and has many attractions, including an inviting bar and a restaurant with their open-air concept allowing for abundant natural light. The rooms all have a view of the sea and provide decent comfort. The hotel also offers a half-board package for an extra charge.

Hotel Club Arenal
$85-$130 all inclusive
≡, ℜ, pb, ☎, ctv, ≈
Avenida de Las Terrazas, Laguna de Boca Ciega
☎97-1272
⇄97-1287
srosso@pantravel.ch

At the gateway to Boca Ciega and by the Río Itabo, the Hotel Club Arenal

Accommodations

stands on a small peninsula surrounded by tropical vegetation. Entirely rebuilt in 1998, the enormous all-inclusive-style 156-room complex has replaced the small Hotel Itabo that once stood here. Very opulent and managed by Italians, the hotel will satisfy even the most discerning guests, with its welcoming staff, spacious rooms, tennis courts, peace and quiet, cleanliness, bars, restaurants and numerous activities.

Hotel Atlántico
$95-$120 all inclusive
≡, ≈, ℜ, pb, ctv
Avenida de las Terrazas no. 21
☎97-1085 to 98
⇄80-3911
The Hotel Atlántico, located opposite, is a relatively

modern, well-kept place with good service. The building faces right onto a section of the beach monitored by a lifeguard. A sports complex (tennis, archery, etc.), several restaurants and a danceclub are also located on the premises.

Villa Los Pinos
$175 for up to four people
≡, ℝ, K, pb, ctv
Avenida las Terrazas
☎97-1361
⇄80-2144
You can also rent a house at the Villa Los Pinos, at the edge of Santa Maria. These fully renovated, two-bedroom houses are located in a peaceful setting near the sea.

Restaurants

You won't have any problems finding a place to eat in Havana; you have the choice of both restaurants and *paladares*.

Restaurants catering to tourists usually provide good food while at other Cuban restaurants, where you pay in *moneda nacional*, you are sure of only one thing: ridiculously cheap prices. *Paladares* are small family restaurants that have a permit to serve about a dozen people. The atmosphere is usually friendly and the food excellent, although they are fairly expensive, considering that a meal costs from $8 to $10. To find a *paladar*, let someone take you to one. Young people are continually on the lookout for tourists to help and will probably approach you in the streets often during your stay.

Note that in addition to the places mentioned in the following pages, there are generally one or more restaurants at most of the hotels.

$	Less than $12
$$	from $12 to $21
$$$	$22 and up

Cuban Cuisine

Cuban cuisine is actually quite succulent. Pork is the

meat of choice, and it is prepared in many different ways (baked, grilled and fried) and is often basted with *mojo*, a sauce with a base of oil, lemon and garlic. Rice, plantain and manioc accompany the meat. *Arroz moro* or *congrí* is a dish that is available in all good Creole restaurants; it consists of rice cooked with black and red beans, onions and spices. Surprisingly, Cubans do not eat much fish. Seafood, including rock lobster, is available in many restaurants.

Food Glossary

Agua	water
Ajo	garlic
Arroz	rice
Batido	beverage made of fruit, ice and milk
Camarone	shrimp
Carne	meat
Carne de res	beef
Cerveza	beer
Chichárron	marinated and cooked meat or chicken
Chivo	goat
Chuleta	cutlet
Conejo	rabbit
Empanadas	small turnovers stuffed with meat or vegetables
Filete	steak
Granadilla	grenadine
Huevo	egg
Jamón	ham
Jugo	juice
Langosta	crayfish
Leche	milk
Limón	lemon
Mariscos	seafood
Mermelada	jam
Naranja	orange
Pan	bread
Papas fritas	fried potatoes (French fries)
Pescado	fish
Piña	pineapple
Plátanos fritos	fried bananas
Pollo	chicken
Pollo frito	fried chicken
Postre	dessert
Queso	cheese
Sopa	soup
Tamarindo	tamarind
Tortilla	omelette
Tostada	toast
Vino	wine
Zanahoria	carrot

Tour A: The Old City

See map p 79

The old city is filled with good restaurants and they have increased in number considerably over the last few years in order to keep up with the growing tourist trade. Some of these new establishments are quite reputable.

So many discoveries await you here... even by simply looking out the window onto the street.
- *P. Escudero*

A peaceful moment, watching the un setting into the sea from a balcony along the Malecón.
- *P. Escudero*

The elegant Vedado neighbourhood is home to superb, richly decorated residences.
- *P. Escudero*

It can be quite pleasant to stroll along the Calle San Rafael in the Centro, a lively neighbourhood where the heart of Havana beats at its own rhythm.
- *Pierre Loubier*

Cafetería Mirador de la Bahía
$
9am to 10pm
Calle Obispo no. 59, between Calle Officios and Calle Baratillo

The view at Cafetería Mirador de la Bahía is unbeatable. It's right in front of Plaza de Armas, on the roof of the former U.S. embassy. The view of the bay from up high is magnificent enough to make you forget the food… In fact, it's better to just have a drink and appreciate the sights. To get to the roof, use the building's main door and take the elevator at the end of the hall.

Los Dos Hermanos
$
open 24hrs
Avenida San Pedro, corner Calle Sol

Located at the end of Alameda de Paula, this friendly little restaurant has been preparing light meals for more than a century. Although its harbour atmosphere is charming, it's quite noisy. The patio is slightly quieter. The menu of chicken, fish and french fries give a good indication of the setting. On the walls of the bar at the restaurant's entrance, a few historical photographs provide an interesting perspective of this area.

Doña Eutimia
$
62 Callejón del Chorro
☎*61-9489*

The most popular *paladar* in the old city is definitely Doña Eutimia, a small, inviting colonial house owned by a sculptor and located at the end of a little dead-end street that branches off the Plaza de la Catedral. The Creole cuisine is succulent, especially the *cerdo asado* (oven-baked pork). Parties of several people are advised to reserve a table, as the place is usually packed. If there's no room, you can try one of the six other *paladares* on the same charming dead-end street.

Café Paris
$
open 24hrs
Calle San Ignacio 202, at Calle Obispo
☎*62-0466*

Also located in the old part of the city, Café Paris serves simple, affordable meals (chicken, pizza, …) and boasts a side counter open around the clock. The place also sometimes features live music, but most of the time it plays recorded Latin music.

Torre de Marfil

$

Tue to Sun noon to 10pm
Calle Mercadares, between Calles
Obispo and Obrapía
☎**57-1038**

For Cantonese food, head
to Torre de Marfil, where
the variety of dishes is
rather amazing. Try the
delicious Cantonese-style
chicken.

La Iluvia de Oro

$

open 24hrs
Calle Obispo 316, at Habana
☎**62-9870**

With its long, seemingly
endless counter, La Iluvia
de Oro is a wonderful place
open 'round the clock. Its
menu offers a variety of
snack food such as chicken,
pizza, sandwiches and
pasta.

Cafetería Torre La Vega

$

Mon to Sat 9am to 7pm
Calle Obrapía 114, between Calle
Officios and Calle Mercaderes

Next to the Casa de Mexico,
the Cafetería Torre La Vega
is the perfect low-budget
alternative. Spaghetti is
served in generous portions
and costs barely $1. But get
there early, because the
place closes as early as
7pm, and customers wish-
ing to take advantage of the
establishment's low prices
must sometimes push their
way through to the counter.

Restaurante Hanoi

$

every day noon to 11pm Calle
Teniente Rey 507, at Calle Bernaza
☎**57-1029**

Despite its name,
Restaurante Hanoi offers
fare that is more Cuban
than Vietnamese, since Vietnamese ingredients are often in short supply here.
The restaurant therefore
offers its patrons a menu of
chicken-, pork- or
meat-based dishes served
with rice and beans. The
place is usually fairly quiet.

Puerto de Sagua

$

noon to midnight
Avenida de Bélica, corner Calle
Acosta
☎**57-1026**

Located next to the railway
station and Casa de Martí,
this restaurant is hard to
miss. It looks like a yellow
and blue boat with port-
holes, which are, in fact,
aquariums. This seafood
restaurant serves a Puerto
de Sagua paella, which at
$10 for two people, is a
true gift from the sea.

El Baturo

$

noon to midnight
Avenida de Bélgica, between Calle
Jesús María and Calle Merced
☎**66-9078**

In this other fish and seafood restaurant, the atmosphere is pleasant and re-

laxed. A good place that's simple and unpretentious.

Gentiluomo
$-$$
noon to midnight
Calle Obispo, corner Calle Berneza
☎57-1299
This affordable Italian restaurant has just opened its doors right behind the Floridita. Portions are generous and the food is delicious. A good spot for pizza or pasta.

Los Marinos
$-$$
noon to midnight
Avenida del Puerto, corner Calle Justiz
☎57-1402
Located just behind Plaza de Armas, Los Marinos serves fish and seafood on a quay that has been transformed into a restaurant. As a result, one has the impression the restaurant is floating on the water. In the evening, with the lights of the bay twinkling all around, the place seems almost surreal.

La Mina
$-$$
open 24hrs
Calle Obispo, corner Calle Officios
☎62-0216
This restaurant seems to occupy a whole section of Plaza de Armas and serves Cuban food in a typical setting. Here also, the location seems to be more important than the food.

Bar Restaurant Cabaña
$$
Calle Cuba no. 12, at the corner of Calle Peña Pobre
☎33-5670
If you've got a big appetite, head to the Bar Restaurant Cabaña for some Creole cuisine. This is a new place whose all-you-can-eat policy has made it an instant hit. It is located on the outskirts of Havana, near the old castle that now serves as a police station. Although the atmosphere is friendly, the service can be a bit rushed.

Castillo de Farnés
$$
open 24 hrs
Calle Monserrate 361, at Calle Obrapia
☎63-1260
Located in the old city, Castillo de Farnés enjoys a reputation that attracts many clients. Decorated like an old English pub, the international cuisine is of good quality and the atmosphere is relaxed, even bohemian.

Restaurante Al Medina
$$
Calle Oficio No. 12, west of Plaza de Armas, between Calle Obispo and Calle Obra pía
☎57-1041
Restaurante Al Medina is tucked away inside the Casa del Arabe, which presents ethnological and cultural exhibitions. Built in 1688 and now completely

restored to its original state, this house is an example of Mozarab architecture. The restaurant is located on the second floor. Decorated with pouffes and cushions in the Arabic tradition, it is flanked by a refreshingly cool mezzanine with vine-covered walls. A veritable oasis, this is the perfect place to escape the rigours of the tropical heat and the hubbub of the city. The Almedina's menu and cuisine are unparalleled in Havana, and the grilled meat dishes are sure to please even the most demanding palate.

D' Giovanni's
$$
Calle Tacón, between Calle Empedrado and Calle O'Reilly
☎57-1036

D'Giovanni's is – surprise, surprise – where lovers of Italian food go to get their fix. The place is friendly and comfortable, and the cuisine rarely disappoints.

La Dominica
$$-$$$
noon to midnight
Calle O'Reilly
corner Calle Mercaderes
☎66-2917

This restaurant's stylish decor is bright and refined. The Italian cuisine is quite delicious and the wine list will satisfy even the most demanding customers.

Café de Oriente
$$$
noon to 1am
Calle Officios, corner Calle Amargura
☎66-6686

Situated right on Plaza de San Francisco, this beautiful restaurant is tastefully decorated. Delicious international cuisine is served in a setting so chic, it is breathtaking. Upstairs, the glass ceiling alone is worth the visit. The wine list is certainly one of the most complete in Havana. The place also has a 24hr bar-café with Cuban music playing every evening. This is the perfect place for those who want to treat themselves to something special.

La Bodeguita del Medio
$$$
Calle Empedrado no. 207
☎33-8276 or 57-1374

La Bodeguita del Medio is a veritable institution of Cuban cuisine, and it is worth coming here just to see the place. In typical Cuban fashion, it is usually packed with tourists inside, with throngs of Cubans posted out front. *Jineteros* hang out on little Calle Empedrado, and you can't walk by without someone asking you for a dollar or a pen, or trying to sell you a box of cigars. There is an extremely festive atmosphere in the restaurant, whose walls are covered with graffiti, signatures, poems and thoughts hand-written by every Tom, Dick and Harry over the years, as well as a few contributions by such famous figures as Ernest Hemingway and Fidel Castro. Hemingway used to come here regularly for a *mojito*, a cocktail made with rum, sugar and mint, so it would be flouting tradition not to try one while you're here. The menu consists of Creole dishes made with pork, rice, black beans and manioc and served with a garlic and oil sauce known as *mojo*. Although the place has a good reputation, its tremendous popularity has had a somewhat negative impact on the quality of the food. Nevertheless, you will rarely be disappointed by a meal at La Bodeguita, and it remains a must in Havana. Don't be shy about clearing your way through the crowd that is perpetually gathered out front, if only to stop by for a *mojito* at the bar.

El Patio
$$$
☎57-1034
Located on Plaza de la Catedral, El Patio is always busy and has a convivial atmosphere. Its roofless courtyard, with its pretty fountain and profusion of tropical plants, will transport you back to colonial times and also offers some shelter from the sun. Musi-

cians liven up the atmosphere both inside the courtyard and out on the terrace on the Plaza de la Catedral. The food is excellent, especially the Creole dishes. If you want to take in the scene on the plaza, you can order from the cafeteria menu on the terrace; the fried chicken makes a great lunch. The terrace is also one of the best places in the old city to enjoy an afternoon cocktail, as long as the crowds of tourists don't bother you.

La Floridita
$$$
at the corner of Calle Obispo and Calle Montserrate
☎33-8856 or 57-1300
A unique gastronomical and historical experience awaits you at La Floridita, by far the most famous restaurant in Havana. Hemingway's very favourite place to eat, La Floridita celebrates all the delicious subtleties of seafood. Its history dates back over 178 years, and it is considered the birthplace of the daiquiri. Ask for the *papa especial*, made with a double shot of rum, the way the famous writer liked it.

Regla and Guanabacoa

Mi Rinconcito
$
noon to midnight
Calle Maceo no. 108, corner Calle La Piedra
Regla
This small *paladar* is right near Galería Taller A. Canet. It is a simple place that serves decent food.

Sylvain Postelería
Calle Pepe Antonio no. 366
Guanabacoa
Situated near Parque Martí, Sylvain Postelería is an amazing pastry shop. All that's missing is croissants.

Tours B and C: The Prado and the Centro

See maps p 107 and p 115

The Prado and Centro are not known for their gourmet food. The *paladares* here are numerous however, particularly in the area by the Prado, and if you stroll along the promenade at dinnertime, someone will probably offer to take you to one of the best places.

Barrio Chino is perhaps the exception in this culinary void. Calle Cuchillo, the little street that runs through Chinatown, is now lined with Chinese restaurants, each with a terrace. The menus are more or less identical and prices are modest. You can easily eat well for less than $5.

El Pacífico
$
noon to 8pm
Calle San Nicolás, at the end of Calle Cuchillo
☎63-3443
El Pacífico probably has the best food of all the restaurants in Chinatown and certainly has the most beautiful decor. This institution is worth the detour.

Oasis
$
Avenida Paseo del Prado no. 258
☎62-6858
The Oasis serves inexpensive cafeteria-style Arabic food and has a pleasant interior courtyard. The bakery's cookies and cakes are very popular with local residents.

Tour D: The Vedado

See map p 147

There are many restaurants in the Vedado, some of which have unfortunately been hard-hit by the country's current economic crisis. It doesn't help that this area is not very popular with tourists. Nevertheless, a few restaurants, several of which have become veritable insititutions of Cuban cuisine over the years, have recovered their former prestige. A number of new places have also opened up, including several charming, quality *paladares*.

Las Tres B
$
noon to midnight
Calle 21, between Calle K and Calle L
☎*32-9276*
Located right behind Parque Coppelia, Las Tres B is a delightful *paladar* that has been serving Creole dishes since 1965. The place is charming and the food delicious.

El Conchinito
$
noon to midnight
La Rampa, between Calle H and Calle I
☎*32-6256*
As its name suggests, this restaurant specializes in

pork dishes. There are two menus, one with the price in dollars and the other in pesos. Try to get the latter if you're on a budget.

Los Sietes Mares
$
10am to 10pm
La Rampa, corner Calle J
☎*31-9226*
Los Sietes Mares is a typical Cuban seafood restaurant. Here, everything is in pesos. The terrace is pleasant and has a very local atmosphere. Fish has pride of place but, as in all exclusively Cuban restaurants, the menu depends on availability.

Cuba 21
$
noon to midnight
Calle 21, corner Calle N
☎*32-9602*
Also called Club 21, this establishment offers a Creole menu in a charming atmosphere. Watch out for the air conditioning however – it keeps the tempera-

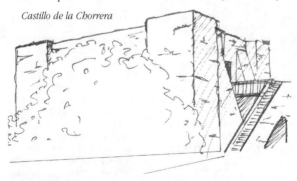

Castillo de la Chorrera

ture at just a few degrees above freezing. Bring warm clothing.

El Mandarín

$

11am to 11pm
Calle 23, corner Calle M
☎*32-0677*

El Mandarín is a Chinese restaurant that Cubans seem to be wild about, judging by the long lineups that stretch down the stairs to the street. This is another place that accepts both dollars and pesos.

Restaurante Pekín

$

noon to midnight
Calle 12, between Calle 21 and La Rampa

Situated at the end of La Rampa near the entrance to Cementerio Cristóbal Colón, this little restaurant seems to be very popular. Chinese meals are served and are payable in pesos. You can have a good meal here for less than a dollar.

Cinecitta

$

noon to midnight
La Rampa, corner Calle 12

This is a family restaurant offering Cuban-style Italian food. The spaghetti is more than acceptable. You often have to wait for a table, but it's certainly worthwhile. It's a good place to go for a snack after the Cine Chaplin.

Doña Yulla
Taberna Don Pepe

$

10am to 11pm
Calle San Lázaro, corner Calle Infanta

These two places serve food to students for a few pesos. The food is excellent and they are good places to have a beer and meet people. Many foreign students eat their meals here.

Restaurante Los Amigos

$

Calle 19, at the corner of Calle M

Located kitty-corner to the Hotel Victoria, this family restaurant lies tucked away at the end of a little lane leading to the back of the house. It is usually crowded with locals, so you might have to wait a few minutes for a table. The Creole cuisine is succulent and served in generous portions, and the prices are unbeatable. This is an excellent place to escape the throngs of tourists and mingle with the locals.

La Carreta

$

every day noon to midnight
at Calle 21 and Avenida K
☎*32-4485*

Right in the middle of the Vedado, La Carreta is a small, unpretentious restaurant where musicians liven up the evenings. The food is typically Cuban, the usual mix of rice, beans, chicken and salad. For those on a tight budget, there is a **cafe-teria** next door that offers a limited menu including delicious ham and cheese sandwiches for only $1 each (for some reason, sandwiches are payable in pesos and drinks in dollars). Watch out for the sub-arctic air conditioning, which can sometimes freeze you in your tracks.

La Roca
$-$$
noon to 4pm, 8pm to 1am
Calle 21, corner Calle M
☎33-4501
This establishment has been open since 1956 and its decor elegantly reflects the modern, slightly kitsch style of the 1950s. International cuisine and seafood are served in a room with large windows tinted numerous colours. The crayfish and shrimps are very fresh because they come from the restaurant's own aquarium. The wine list is above average.

La Cosona del 17
$-$$
noon to midnight
Calle 17 no. 60, between Calle M and Calle N
☎33-4529
This beautiful former residence was built in 1921 and once belonged to Fidel's godfather, according to the restaurant's management. Upstairs, there is a lovely terrace where you can people-watch while enjoy-

ing delicious food. Chicken is the house specialty. Charming, attractive decor.

Mesón de la Chorrera
$-$$
11am to midnight
Calle Calzada no. 1252, corner Calle 20
☎33-4521
Right next to restaurant 1830 (see below) and under the same management, Mesón de la Chorrera serves Creole food in an atmosphere that is hard to beat. The restaurant is on the second floor of Castillo de la Chorrera, a 17th-century fort built to guard the entrance of the small bay into which flows the Río Almendares. The cannons remain in the dining room – they still point menacingly through the loopholes. A delightful terrace has been set up outside at the base of the fort.

1830
$$
Calzada no. 1252
Located at the mouth of the Río Almendares, at the west end of the Malecón, 1830 boasts an enchanting oceanside setting. Its extravagant stone architecture is complemented by Japanese-style landscaping, complete with terraces, fountains and foot bridges, making you feel as if you've stepped into a fairytale. The Creole cuisine is decent, and the seafood dishes are espe-

cially recommended. What
you'll remember most is the
extraordinary ambiance and
magical setting.

El Conejito
$$
Calle M, at the corner of Calle 17
☎*32-4671*
One of the traditional res-
taurants in this area, El
Conejito, is modelled after a
16th-century English tavern.
As its name suggests, it
serves rabbit dishes.

La Torre
$$
Calle 17 no. 155, at the corner of Calle
M
☎*32-4630*
La Torre, located on the
35th floor of the FOCSA
building, offers a stunning
panoramic view of the city.
The food is not on par with
the view, however, so stop
by for drinks or coffee instead.

Castillo de Jagüa
$$
3pm to 2am, closed Mon
Calle 23, at Avenida G
Castillo de Jagüa is a charm-
ing little bar-restaurant that
features both Cuban and
international cuisine. A
young university crowd
gathers here in an unpre-
tentious setting. You can
pay in either pesos or dol-
lars, depending on how
glaringly obvious a gringo
you are.

Monseigneur
$$-$$$
every day noon to 2am
Calle 21, at Avenida O
☎*32-9884*
Opposite the Hotel
Nacional is the Monsei-
gneur, a State-owned res-
taurant specializing in inter-
national cuisine but also
offering a good variety of
seafood dishes (try the
freshly caught shrimp,
yum!). Prices are reason-
able.

Tour E: Miramar

See map p 129

Miramar has very good res-
taurants but most are quite
expensive.

Vistamar
$
noon to midnight
Avenida 1, between Calle 22 and Calle
24
☎*23-8328*
An attractive *paladar*,
Vistamar has a fabulous
view of the sea. The place
is friendly and the food
delicious. It is the ideal
place for people who like a
family atmosphere.

Lisboa
$
noon to 10pm
Avenida 1, corner Calle 42
Despite its name, Lisboa
serves Italian food. Facing
the sea and unpretentious,

Restaurants

it is a little less expensive than other restaurants in the area, which should suit people travelling on a tight budget.

🦐 Don Cangrejo
$$
noon to midnight
Avenida 1, between Calle 16 and Calle 18
☎24-4169

Directly overlooking the sea, Don Cangrejo is an excellent seafood restaurant. The view is worth the price of the food, especially if you sit upstairs. The wine cellar is adequate, and for the price, it's hard to find a better place.

Dos Gardenias, Gambinas, Shangai
$$
noon to midnight
Avenida 7, corner Calle 6
☎24-2353

Right near El Aljibe is a large house dating from the 1940s with three restaurants under the same roof. The first serves Creole food on a beautiful exterior patio; the second is a Neapolitan-style Italian restaurant with red-and-white-checked tablecloths; and the third, which we are unsure about, has a Chinese menu. All three seem very good and attract passing tourists.

Le Sélect
$$
noon to midnight
Avenida 5, between Calle 28 and Calle 30
☎24-7410

Located in a very beautiful house built in the late 1940s, Le Sélect, behind the *tienda*, offers an international menu fit for the most refined palates.

Quinta y 16
$$
noon to midnight
Avenida 5, corner Calle 16
☎24-1185

Serving international and Creole cuisine on a lovely terrace where you can watch the food being prepared, Quinta y 16 is one of the most delightful places in Miramar. And if you feel like smoking after the meal, there is a cigar store on the premises.

El Aljibe
$$
every day noon to midnight
Calle 7, between Avenidas 24 and 26
☎24-1583

El Aljibe offers an excellent *criollo* menu. Tourists and Cuban high society gather here beneath thatched roofs to savour chicken-based specialties. The service is flawless and the quality of the food leaves no one indifferent.

La Maison
$$-$$$
noon to 1am
Calle 16 no. 701, corner Avenida 7
☎ *24-7411*
The large former homes of
the rich bourgeoisie have
become fashionable over
the last few years. These
dwellings from the 1940s
are being transformed into
a mixture of *tiendas*, restaurants and bars. La Maison is
unquestionably the most
notable of its kind. How-
ever, it is better known for
its fashion shows than its
food, which seems quite
ordinary.

El Tocororo
$$$
Calle 18, at the corner of Avenida 3
☎ *24-2209 or 24-4530*
El Tocororo is original on
all scores. Named after the
national bird of Cuba, it has
an extravagant decor featur-
ing a blend of tropical am-
biance, graffiti and fake
tocororos. The menu is just
as creative, and the food is
lovingly prepared. Very chic
and expensive.

La Ferminia
$$$
Avenida 5 no. 8807, between Calle 182
and Calle 184
☎ *24-6555*
La Ferminia is not only one
of the best restaurants in
Cuba, but also one of the
loveliest. Once a private
home, it has numerous individual rooms, each able to

accommodate from 10 to 30
people. These rooms are
decorated with Louis XV
furniture and furniture
made of *caoba*, a precious
Cuban wood. Three out
door terraces enable diners
to feast in the ambiance of
their choice. The restaurant
also offers courses in gourmet cooking and hotel
management, so naturally
the service is excellent and
courteous. The mixed grill,
meat dishes and seafood
are house specialties. The
maitre d' will be happy to
give you a tour of the premises.

La Cecilia
$$$
Avenida 5 no. 11010, between Calle
110 and Calle 111
☎ *24-1562*
La Cecilia, considered one
of the finest restaurants in
Havana, is named after a
novel by Cuban author
Cirilo Villaverde. Luxuriant
tropical plants adorn the
entrance and the dining
room at the back lies under
two marquees made of Af-
rican wood, creating a
peaceful, inviting atmo-
sphere. Seafood and *criollo*
dishes are the house spe-
cialties. The restaurant has
an excellent wine cellar and
a very competent staff, and
has recently started hosting
a cabaret show on a large
stage surrounded by tropi-
cal trees (*$3; Wed to Mon;*

outdoor *shows* starting at
10pm).

Tour F: The Hemingway Tour

Las Terrazas
$$$
Calle Real no. 161, between Calle Río
and Calle Montaña
☎65-3471
The port town of Cojimar
has an excellent seafood
restaurant, Las Terrazas, a
favourite with Hemingway
and his skipper, Gregorio
Fuentes. The latter, the hero
of *The Old Man and the Sea*,
is still alive, and you can
find him here at lunchtime.
Although he is now 98
years old, he can still tell
you all sorts of anecdotes
about Hemingway. As far as
the seafood is concerned,
the baked *paella* is recom-
mended.

Tour G: The Southern Parks

The **Restaurante Ecológico** *($$)*
lies in front of the falls in
the Japanese garden at the
Jardín Botanico. Most of the
dishes served on this attractive terrace, where you can
cool off a bit when the
weather is hot, are vegetar-
ian. The quality of the food
is somewhat uneven, con-
sidering the prices. You
might opt instead for the

Restaurante El Ranchón *($$)*,
which serves a Creole buf-
fet in a lovely rustic house –
the same kind that is used
for drying tobacco leaves –
topped with a roof made of
palm fronds. This restaurant
is set in a forest of pine
trees, a species commonly
found in Cuba, but rare in
the Caribbean as a whole.

Tour H: The Eastern Beaches

Guanabo Club
$
Calle 468, between Calle 3
and Calle 15
☎87-2884
Set on the hilltop in
Guanabo, the Guanabo
Club boasts a gorgeous
view of the little town and
the sea. The clientele con-
sists mainly of vacationing
Cuban soldiers, as there is a
military leisure camp
nearby. The atmosphere is
relaxed early in the eve-
ning, but it gets very lively
later when the danceclub
opens and the crowds of
foreign tourists arrive.

Restaurants

Entertainment

H avana, the cultural
capital of Cuba, has something for
every taste.

I ts urbanity and status in
the Latin American world
make it a choice place for
any cultural activity.

T hings change quickly in
Havana. To find out
what's going on in the city,
read *Cartelera*, a free weekly
newspaper available in
most of the large hotels, or
listen to Radio Taino 93.3,
every day from 5pm to 7pm
for the bilingual (Spanish-
English) cultural program.
This should give you all the
necessary information.

Events

Havana's largest festivals
are the **International Latin
American Film Festival**, which
is held in December, and
the **International Jazz Festival**,
which takes place during
the first week of February.

Since its inception in 1979,
the International Latin
American Film Festival has
become a privileged place
for filmmakers and film
enthusiasts to meet and
exchange ideas. The festival
takes place around Ha-
vana's cinematheque, the
Cine Chaplin, and presents
an array of new films as
well as some retrospectives.
Everyone from Latin-Amer-

ica comes here to show their films.

Havana's International Jazz Festival follows a few weeks later and all the city's concert halls are filled to hear the best jazz Cuba has to offer. For a number of years, international artists have been playing here, which adds to the city's liveliness during these wonderful days. Ticket prices are quite high and the festival is definitively addressed to an elite audience but nevertheless, it should not to be missed by fans of Cuban music and jazz in general.

Two other festivals that are worth mentioning are the **Guaracha Festival**, which takes place in November and showcases traditional music, and the **International Folklore Festival**, which is staged in May.

Havana also has its **carnival**, which takes place during the first weeks of January around the Prado and along the Malecón. Abandoned during the first years of the *periodo especial*, it has since returned in full force. The most interesting aspect is the procession of the *comparsas*, traditional dance groups accompanied by percussive music inspired by African rhythms. With music, colour, dancing and allegorical floats, there is something for everyone.

Cultural Activities

Casa de las Américas
10am to 10pm
Calle G, corner Calle 3
Vedado
☎*55-2706*
Casa de las Américas regularly exhibits work by Latin American artists and organizes symposiums on subjects related to Cuban and Spanish-American culture. This is one of the most important places in the city for the presentation of Cuban culture and everyone is welcome.

Bars and Nightclubs

Tour A: The Old City

Old Havana, including the Parque Central district, is the best area to hear real Cuban music. Everywhere, on terraces, in cafés, hotels and restaurants, groups of musicians share their love of the island's rhythms. All you have to do is follow the music and let your ears decide where to stop.

Casa de la Cultura Julián del Casal

Calle Aguiar, between Calle Amargura and Calle Teniente Rey

Casa de la Cultura Julián del Casal is a cultural centre presenting Cuban music or dances almost every evening. Stop by to find out what's on the program.

Tour D: The Vedado

The Vedado has better venues for Cuban jazz or modern salsa fans.

Copa Room
$25
at Calle Paseo
and the Malecón Vedado
☎33-4051

The Copa Room, formerly known as the Palacio de la Salsa, is a must for salsa lovers. Variety shows are featured here on a regular basis. Call to inquire about the program.

Habana Café
in the Hotel Melia Cohiba

Right next door, the Habana Café is a very popular spot and a venue for musical performances you are sure to enjoy. A memorable evening for Cuban music lovers.

Salón Rojo
10:30pm to 4am
Calle 21, corner Calle N
☎33-3747

Salón Rojo is the old casino at the Hotel Capri. In the evening, this nightclub is more popular with tourists than with city residents.

One of the hottest salsa places in town is the **Café Cantante** *(cover charge; at Paseo and Calle 39, near the bus station, ☎33-5713)* in the Teatro Nacional de Cuba.

For those who prefer jazz to salsa, there are two excellent spots in the Vedado.

La Zorra y El Cuervo
$5
every day 9pm to 3am
155 Calle 23,
between Avenidas N and O
☎66-2407

La Zorra y El Cuervo presents established musicians and new talent every night of the week. Simply go down the small stairway that serves as an entrance and you will fall right into the intimate universe of Latin jazz. Though shows start at 9pm, it's a good two hours before things really get cooking.

Jazz Café
free admission
every evening, 9pm to 3am
Avenida 1, corner Paseo

A pleasant, airy place, Jazz Café is situated on the second floor of Galeria de Paseo, a shopping centre near Hotel Melia Cohiba. The groups that play here are excellent and the atmosphere is laid-back. Definitely a good spot.

Tour E: Miramar

If you're a bit of a romantic soul, you'll love **Dos Gardenias** *(Avenida 7, at the corner of Calle 26)*, where live musicians play the languorous boleros that were all the rage in Latin America back in the 1940s and 1950s. The place is pretty kitschy, and in between the romantic songs, you'll probably have a hard time smothering a smile. The Dos Gardenias has a tiny, intimate room known as **El Salón del Bolero**, which is perfect for incurable romantics. Love lost and rekindled, jealousy, hidden passions... *toda la noche cabe en un bolero* (the whole night is contained in a bolero). At midnight, the *descarga* begins, and various singers and musicians join the featured group.

Salón Rosado Benny More
$10
10pm to 4am
Avenida 41, corner Calle 46
Playa
☎*29-0985* or *23-5322*
This seems to be the best place for dancing, not only in Miramar, but in all Havana. Cubans come to the huge terrace here and let loose to the best modern salsa, played by the country's finest groups.

Havana Club
$10
Mar and Calle 84, Miramar
☎*22-5511*
The Hotel Commodoro has the only trendy mega-danceclub in Havana. The atmosphere at the Havana Club is electrifying night after night, and even if you only hit the town once during your stay, this is the best place to go. Crowds of *Habaneros*, men and women alike, wait at the door to be invited inside, and large numbers of gays turn out on Monday nights.

Tropicana
$50
Calle 72 and Avenida 45
The Tropicana, located in the Marianao area, presents the most spectacular and celebrated cabaret show in all of Cuba. Although the entrance charge is prohibitive, you won't be disappointed by the colourful, red-hot performance. On an outdoor stage, thousands of dancers will sweep you up in a

whirlwind of feathers and exoticism.

Tour H: The Eastern Beaches

Guanimar
cover charge
Thu to Sun 9pm to 2am
Avenida 5, between Calles 466 and 468
Guanabo
☎96-2947
The beach area does not have many nightclubs. We suggest the Guanimar, a good place that often puts on salsa shows.

Performing Arts

Gran Teatro de La Habana
Avenida Paseo del Prado
at the corner of Calle San Rafael
☎61-3078
The magnificent Gran Teatro de La Habana, located in front of Parque Central, attests to Havana's rich tradition of theatre and ballet. It is popularly known as the Teatro García Lorca, since its main theatre is named after the celebrated Spanish poet.

El Sótano
Calle K, between Calle 25 and Calle 27
☎32-0632
Theatre lovers interested in discovering contemporary Cuban plays should head to El Sótano.

Guiñol
Calle M, between Calles 19 and 21
☎32-6262 or 32-8292
The kids will enjoy a trip to the Guiñol to see a puppet show.

Mella
Avenida 1
between Calles 8 and 10
☎32-8696 or 32-5651
The Mella presents performances of modern and folk dance, as well as variety shows.

Teatro Nacional
Calle Paseo, at the corner of Calle 39
on the Plaza de la Revolución
☎79-6011
The decidedly modern Teatro Nacional presents classical music concerts, plays and national and international variety shows. This is where the city's symphony orchestra performs.

Sala-Teatro Hubert de Blanck
Calle Calzada, between Calles A and B
Vedado
☎30-1011
The Sala-Teatro Hubert de Blanck hosts many excellent concerts of both classical and contemporary music.

Teatro Karl Marx
Avenida 1, between Calles 8 and 10
☎30-0720 or 30-5521
In Miramar, the Teatro Karl Marx is a very large, modern theatre where national and international variety shows are presented.

Entertainment

Movie Theatres

Cubans are avid moviegoers. In Havana, there are cinemas everywhere, usually showing Cuban or Spanish films, or vapid Hollywood films.

Cine Chaplin
Calle 23 no. 1155, between Calle 11 and Calle 12
☎*31-1101*
Havana's cinematheque, the Cine Chaplin, is the place for those with a need to see a good film. International films are shown here (two showings, at 5pm and 8pm, every day except Tuesday). The International Latin American Film Festival in Havana revolves around this cinema every year in December.

Sports

Baseball is certainly the most popular sport in Cuba, and Havana is no exception. The city has two teams that play regularly, but it is the matches between Havana and Santiago de Cuba that attract the crowds. These games are held in the **Estadio Latinoamericano in Cerro**. This huge stadium, with a seating capacity of 60,000, is an ideal place to experience some Havana life. To find out when the games take place, ask a local; almost everyone seems to know.

Street Baseball

Habaneros are known for their ingenuity. So to take advantage of their favourite sport in the city's narrow streets, they have developed a completely original way of playing baseball. There does not seem to be any rule for the number of players. But what is certain is that the ball is hit with an open hand, that there are only two goals, delimited by each side of the street, and that it is necessary to pass between them to avoid being automatically disqualified. If you walk around the Centro during the weekend, you are sure to see a game of urban baseball.

Shopping

More and more shops are opening in Havana, and shopaholics, who were often disappointed by the city in the past, are beginning to find things more to their liking.

What should you buy? Well, the brand-name Cuban cigars sold in specialty shops are always a good deal, since they are twice as expensive outside of Cuba. People in the street will probably try to sell you black-market cigars. Eighty percent of the time, these products are not authentic. Although many cigar smokers won't notice the difference, true aficionados are sure to be disappointed. The prices may be higher in specialty shops, but are guaranteed to be quality cigars that have been stored in ideal conditions.

Capitolio) has an excellent selection of cigars and offers tours of the factory. Cigars are also sold in most more hotels in Havana.

Cigars

La Casa Partagás (*Calle Industria No. 520, behind the*

Clothing

In terms of clothing, Havana (and Cuba in general) is not the best place to buy a new wardrobe. There are, however, a few exclusive boutiques along the central hallway of the **Hotel Sevilla** *(Calle Trocadero No. 55)*, near the Paseo del Prado in Old Havana.

El Quitrín
Calle Obispo and Calle San Juan
Old Havana
El Quitrín is a workshop where lace is hand-made. It is worth coming here just to see the people at work, not to mention the flawless and unique finished products.

La Maison *(Calle 16, at the corner of Avenida 7, in Miramar)* in Miramar specializes in women's fashions and has the best selection of handbags, accessories and exclusive clothing by Cuban fashion designers. Fashion shows are held here regularly. A few shops at the **Marina Hemingway** also have an interesting selection of casual sportswear and eveningwear.

Crafts

Local arts and crafts are sometime interesting; here you will find such things as lovely wooden sculptures and clay pots.

There are three large craft markets in Havana. In the Vedado the well-known

market that used to be held on Calle G has moved to the Malécon, between Calles N and O and on Calle 23. You can browse through a vast array of local crafts here from Tuesday to Sunday until sunset. You'll also pass by the craftspeople from the Plaza de la Catedral market, which is now by the sea in front of the Seminario San Carlos and is held every day, except Sunday. Numerous vendors sell a wide range of crafts and books on the square and along the adjacent streets.

Lastly, another craft market has been set up in the Vedado at the corner of Calle D, between Calle 1 and Calle 3. **Mercado D y Malecón** has lower prices than the other two markets.

The **Palacio de l'Artesania** *(Calle Cuba No. 64, Old Havana)* has an excellent selection of crafts and an entire section devoted to music (tapes and CDs) as well as many instruments traditionally used by Cuban musicians. In general, the crafts are priced slightly higher than at the local markets. However, if you have a little time and money to spare, this is a great place to find top-quality pieces.

Art Galleries

Since the government has forbidden the export of its cultural property, make sure to obtain a certificate from the Fondo de Bienes Culturales if you buy a major work, such as a large painting, to make sure it won't be seized at the border when you leave. In Havana, the Fondo is located in the La Casona art gallery (see below).

Galería La Casona
Mon to Fri 10am to 4pm
Calle Muralla No. 107
at the corner of Calle San Ignacio
☎*62-2633* or *61-2875*
The Galería La Casona in the old city is also the parent institution of the Cuban Cultural Heritage Fund. Located in a large colonial house, it sells sculptures, paintings and ceramics by Cuban artists.

Galería Forma
Calle Obispo No. 255
between Calle Cuba and Calle Aguiar
Old Havana
☎*62-2103*

Galería La Acacia
Mon to Sat 10am to 4pm
Calle Sain José No. 114
between Calle Industria and Calle Consulado, Centro Habana
☎*63-9364*
Galería La Acacia sells works by the greatest Cuban artists of all time.

Fans of contemporary Latin American art will enjoy visiting the **Casa de las Américas**, a large cultural organization that houses the **Galería de Arte Haydée Santamaria** *($2; Mon to Fri 10am to 4:30pm; Calle G, at the corner of Avenida 3, Vedado,* ☎*32-3587,* ≠*32-7272, casa@tinored.cu).*

Shopping Centres

Summer clothing, shoes, food, electronic merchandise, household appliances – you'll find it all at the **Centro Comercial 5ta y 42** *(Avenida 5, at the corner of Calle 42)* in Miramar. This is the largest shopping centre in Havana, but is still small by North American standards. It is an excellent place to run errands, or to buy fresh French bread and other specialties. There are cafeterias where you can grab a soft drink or a slice of pizza to fortify yourself before hitting the stores again.

Supermarkets

Supermarkets have been popping up here and there in Havana since U.S. currency was legalized. They are usually open Monday to Saturday from 9am to 5pm and Sunday from 9am to noon. Here are a few:

Shopping

Tour A: The Old City

Mercado Bellamar
Calle Prado and Calle Dragones
☎*33-8328*

Tour C: The Centro

Supermercado Amistad
Calle San-Lazaro and Calle Infanta
☎*33-5832*

Tour D: The Vedado

Mercado Carimar
4 Calle D
☎*33-3879*

Tour E: Miramar

Supermercado 3ra y 70
Avenida 3 and Calle 70
☎*33-2890*

Farmers' Markets

As a result of one of the government's recent economic reforms, farmer's markets have sprung up all over the country. Havana has a large number of these *mercados agropecuarios*, commonly known as *agros*, where all transactions are made in Cuban currency. Although the choice is generally limited, these are the best places to buy fruits and vegetables at ridiculously low prices. It is worth visiting the local *agros*, if only to immerse yourself in the everyday life of the city's residents, far from the touristy areas.

You'll find a typical *agromercado* in the Barrio Chino (Chinatown), which is located in Centro Habana. This market has the largest selection of spices in all Havana. The *agromercado* in Nuevo Vedado *(Calle Tulipán, near the Estación de Trenes 19 de Noviembre)* offers an uneven selection of fruit and vegetables, which varies from season to season. Nevertheless, it is usually crowded, making it a great place to take some photos.

Glossary

Pronunciation

Consonants

b	Is pronounced **b** or sometimes a soft **v**, depending on the region or the person: *bizcocho* (biz-koh-choh or viz-koh-choh).
c	As in English, *c* is pronounced as **s** before *i* and *e*: *cerro* (seh-rroh). When it is placed in front of other vowels, it is hard and pronounced as **k**: *carro* (kah-rroh). The *c* is also hard when it comes before a consonant, except before an *h* (see further below).
d	Is pronounced like a soft **d**: *dar* (dahr). *D* is usually not pronounced when at the end of a word.
g	As with the *c*, *g* is soft before an *i* or an *e*, and is pronounced like a soft **h**: *gente* (hente). In front of other vowels and consonants, the *g* is hard: *golf* (pronounced the same way as in English).
ch	Is pronounced **ch**, as in English: *leche* (le-che). Like the *ll*, this combination is considered a single letter in the Spanish alphabet, listed separately in dictionaries and telephone directories.
h	Is not pronounced: *hora* (oh-ra).
j	Is pronounced like a guttural **h**, as in "him".

Glossary

ll	Is pronounced like a hard **y**, as in "yes": *llamar* (yah-mar). In some regions, such as central Colombia, *ll* is pronounced as a soft **g**, as in "mirage" (*Medellín* is pronounced Medegin). Like the *ch*, this combination is considered a single letter in the Spanish alphabet, and is listed separately in dictionaries and telephone directories.
ñ	Is pronounced like the **ni** in "onion", or the **ny** in "canyon": *señora* (seh-nyo-rah).
qu	Is pronounced **k**: *aquí* (ah-kee).
r	Is rolled, as the Irish or Italian pronunciation of **r**.
s	Is always pronounced **s** like "sign": *casa* (cah-ssah).
v	Is pronounced like a **b**: *vino* (bee-noh).
z	Is pronounced like **s**: *paz* (pahss).

Vowels

a	Is always pronounced **ah** as in "part", and never *ay* as in "day": *faro* (fah-roh).
e	Is pronounced **eh** as in "elf," and never *ey* as in "grey or "ee" as in "key": *helado* (eh-lah-doh].
i	Is always pronounced **ee**: *cine* (see-neh).
o	Is always pronounced **oh** as in "cone": *copa* (koh-pah).
u	Is always pronounced **oo**: *universidad* (oo-nee-ver-see-dah).

All other letters are pronounced the same as in English.

Stressing Syllables

In Spanish, syllables are differently stressed. This stress is very important, and emphasizing the right syllable might even be necessary to make yourself understood. If a vowel has an accent, this syllable is the one that should be stressed. If there is no accent, follow this rule:

Stress the second-last syllable of any word that ends with a vowel: *ami*go.

Stress the last syllable of any word that ends in a consonant, except for **s** (plural of nouns and adjectives) or **n** (plural of nouns): *usted* (but *ami*gos, *ha*blan).

A Few Expressions

Greetings

Goodbye	*adiós, hasta luego*
Good afternoon and good evening	*buenas tardes*
Hi (casual)	*hola*
Good morning	*buenos días*
Good night	*buenas noches*
Thank-you	*gracias*
Please	*por favor*
You are welcome	*de nada*
Excuse me	*perdone/a*
My name is...	*mi nombre es...*
What is your name?	*¿cómo se llama usted?*
no/yes	*no/sí*
Do you speak English?	*¿habla usted inglés?*
Slower, please	*más despacio, por favor*
I am sorry, I don't speak Spanish	*Lo siento, no hablo español*
How are you?	*¿qué tal?*
I am fine	*estoy bien*
I am American (male/female)	*Soy estadounidense*
I am Australian	*Soy autraliano/a*
I am Belgian	*Soy belga*
I am British (male/female)	*Soy británico/a*
I am Canadian	*Soy canadiense*

I am German (male/female)	*Soy alemán/a*
I am Italian (male/female)	*Soy italiano/a*
I am Swiss	*Soy suizo*
I am a tourist	*Soy turista*
single (m/f)	*soltero/a*
divorced (m/f)	*divorciado/a*
married (m/f)	*casado/a*
friend (m/f)	*amigo/a*
child (m/f)	*niño/a*
husband, wife	*esposo/a*
mother, father	*madre, padre*
brother, sister	*hermano/a*
widower widow	*viudo/a*
I am hungry	*tengo hambre*
I am ill	*estoy enfermo/a*
I am thirsty	*tengo sed*

Directions

beside	*al lado de*
to the right	*a la derecha*
to the left	*a la izquierda*
here, there	*aquí, allí*
into, inside	*dentro*
outside	*fuera*
behind	*detrás*
in front of	*delante*
between	*entre*
far from	*lejos de*
Where is ... ?	*¿dónde está ... ?*
To get to ...?	*¿para ir a...?*
near	*cerca de*
straight ahead	*todo recto*

Money

money	*dinero / plata*
credit card	*tarjeta de crédito*
exchange	*cambio*
traveller's cheque	*cheque de viaje*
I don't have any money	*no tengo dinero*
The bill, please	*la cuenta, por favor*
receipt	*recibo*

Shopping

store	*tienda*
market	*mercado*
open, closed	*abierto/a, cerrado/a*
How much is this?	*¿cuánto es?*
to buy, to sell	*comprar*, vender
the customer	*el / la cliente*
salesman	*vendedor*
saleswoman	*vendedora*
I need...	*necesito...*
I would like...	*yo quisiera...*
batteries	*pilas*
blouse	*blusa*
cameras	*cámaras*
cosmetics and perfumes	*cosméticos y perfumes*
cotton	*algodón*
dress jacket	*saco*
eyeglasses	*lentes, gafas*
fabric	*tela*
film	*película*
gifts	*regalos*
gold	*oro*
handbag	*bolsa*
hat	*sombrero*
jewellery	*joyería*
leather	*cuero, piel*
local crafts	*artesanía*
magazines	*revistas*
newpapers	*periódicos*
pants	*pantalones*
records, cassettes	*discos, casetas*
sandals	*sandalias*
shirt	*camisa*
shoes	*zapatos*
silver	*plata*
skirt	*falda*
sun screen products	*productos solares*
T-shirt	*camiseta*
watch	*reloj*
wool	*lana*

Miscellaneous

a little	*poco*
a lot	*mucho*
good (m/f)	*bueno/a*
bad (m/f)	*malo/a*
beautiful (m/f)	*hermoso/a*
pretty (m/f)	*bonito/a*
ugly	*feo*
big	*grande*
tall (m/f)	*alto/a*
small (m/f)	*pequeño/a*
short (length) (m/f)	*corto/a*
short (person) (m/f)	*bajo/a*
cold (m/f)	*frío/a*
hot	*caliente*
dark (m/f)	*oscuro/a*
light (colour)	*claro*
do not touch	*no tocar*
expensive (m/f)	*caro/a*
cheap (m/f)	*barato/a*
fat (m/f)	*gordo/a*
slim, skinny (m/f)	*delgado/a*
heavy (m/f)	*pesado/a*
light (weight) (m/f)	*ligero/a*
less	*menos*
more	*más*
narrow (m/f)	*estrecho/a*
wide (m/f)	*ancho/a*
new (m/f)	*nuevo/a*
old (m/f)	*viejo/a*
nothing	*nada*
something (m/f)	*algo/a*
quickly	*rápidamente*
slowly (m/f)	*despacio/a*
What is this?	*¿qué es esto?*
when?	*¿cuando?*
where?	*¿dónde?*

Time

in the afternoon, early evening	*por la tarde*
at night	*por la noche*
in the daytime	*por el día*
in the morning	*por la mañana*

minute	*minuto*
month	*mes*
ever	*jamás*
never	*nunca*
now	*ahora*
today	*hoy*
yesterday	*ayer*
tomorrow	*mañana*
What time is it?	*¿qué hora es?*
hour	*hora*
week	*semana*
year	*año*
Sunday	*domingo*
Monday	*lunes*
Tuesday	*martes*
Wednesday	*miércoles*
Thursday	*jueves*
Friday	*viernes*
Saturday	*sábado*
January	*enero*
February	*febrero*
March	*marzo*
April	*abril*
May	*mayo*
June	*junio*
July	*julio*
August	*agosto*
September	*septiembre*
October	*octubre*
November	*noviembre*
December	*diciembre*

Weather

It is cold	*hace frío*
It is warm	*hace calor*
It is very hot	*hace mucho calor*
sun	*sol*
It is sunny	*hace sol*
It is cloudy	*está nublado*
rain	*lluvia*
It is raining	*está lloviendo*
wind	*viento*
It is windy	*hay viento*
snow	*nieve*

damp	*húmedo*
dry	*seco*
storm	*tormenta*
hurricane	*huracán*

Communication

air mail	*correos aéreo*
collect call	*llamada por cobrar*
dial the number	*marcar el número*
area code, country code	*código*
envelope	*sobre*
long distance	*larga distancia*
post office	*correo*
rate	*tarifa*
stamps	*estampillas*
telegram	*telegrama*
telephone book	*un guia telefónica*
wait for the tone	*esperar la señal*

Activities

beach	*playa*
museum or gallery	*museo*
scuba diving	*buceo*
to swim	*bañarse*
to walk around	*pasear*
hiking	*caminata*
trail	*pista, sendero*
cycling	*ciclismo*
fishing	*pesca*

Transportation

arrival, departure	*llegada, salida*
on time	*a tiempo*
cancelled (m/f)	*anulado/a*
one way ticket	*ida*
return	*regreso*
round trip	*ida y vuelta*
schedule	*horario*
baggage	equipajes
north, south	*norte, sur*
east, west	*este, oeste*
avenue	avenida
street	*calle*
highway	carretera
expressway	*autopista*

airplane	*avión*
airport	*aeropuerto*
bicycle	*bicicleta*
boat	*barco*
bus	*bus*
bus stop	*parada*
bus terminal	*terminal*
train	*tren*
train crossing	*crucero ferrocarril*
station	*estación*
neighbourhood	*barrio*
collective taxi	*colectivo*
corner	*esquina*
express	*rápido*
safe	*seguro/a*
be careful	*cuidado*
car	*coche, carro*
To rent a car	*alquilar un auto*
gas	*gasolina*
gas station	*gasolinera*
no parking	*no estacionar*
no passing	*no adelantar*
parking	*parqueo*
pedestrian	*peaton*
road closed, no through traffic	*no hay paso*
slow down	*reduzca velocidad*
speed limit	*velocidad permitida*
stop	*alto*
stop! (an order)	*pare*
traffic light	*semáforo*

Accommodation

cabin, bungalow	*cabaña*
accommodation	*alojamiento*
double, for two people	*doble*
single, for one person	*sencillo*
high season	*temporada alta*
low season	*temporada baja*
bed	*cama*
floor (first, second...)	*piso*
main floor	*planta baja*
manager	*gerente, jefe*
double bed	*cama matrimonial*

cot	*camita*
bathroom	*baños*
with private bathroom	*con baño privado*
hot water	*agua caliente*
breakfast	*desayuno*
elevator	*ascensor*
air conditioning	*aire acondicionado*
fan	*ventilador, abanico*
pool	*piscina, alberca*
room	*habitación*

Numbers

1	*uno*
2	*dos*
3	*tres*
4	*cuatro*
5	*cinco*
6	*seis*
7	*siete*
8	*ocho*
9	*nueve*
10	*diez*
11	*once*
12	*doce*
13	*trece*
14	*catorce*
15	*quince*
16	*dieciséis*
17	*diecisiete*
18	*dieciocho*
19	*diecinueve*
20	*veinte*
21	*veintiuno*
22	*veintidós*
23	*veintitrés*
24	*veinticuatro*
25	*veinticinco*
26	*veintiséis*
27	*veintisiete*
28	*veintiocho*
29	*veintinueve*
30	*treinta*
31	*treinta y uno*
32	*treinta y dos*

40	*cuarenta*
50	*cincuenta*
60	*sesenta*
70	*setenta*
80	*ochenta*
90	*noventa*
100	*cien*
101	*ciento uno*
102	*ciento dos*
200	*doscientos*
300	*trescientos*
400	*quatrocientoa*
500	*quinientos*
600	*seiscientos*
700	*setecientos*
800	*ochocientos*
900	*novecientos*
1,000	*mil*
1,100	*mil cien*
1,200	*mil doscientos*
2000	*dos mil*
3000	*tres mil*
10,000	*diez mil*
100,000	*cien mil*
1,000,000	*un millón*

Index

Index

Index

Order Form

Ulysses Travel Guides

☐ Acapulco	$14.95 CAN $9.95 US
☐ Atlantic Canada	$24.95 CAN $17.95 US
☐ Bahamas	$24.95 CAN $17.95 US
☐ Beaches of Maine	$12.95 CAN $9.95 US
☐ Bed & Breakfasts in Québec	$14.95 CAN $10.95 US
☐ Belize	$16.95 CAN $12.95 US
☐ Calgary	$17.95 CAN $12.95 US
☐ Canada	$29.95 CAN $21.95 US
☐ Chicago	$19.95 CAN $14.95 US
☐ Chile	$27.95 CAN $17.95 US
☐ Colombia	$29.95 CAN $21.95 US
☐ Costa Rica	$27.95 CAN $19.95 US
☐ Cuba	$24.95 CAN $17.95 US
☐ Dominican Republic	$24.95 CAN $17.95 US
☐ Ecuador and Galapagos Islands	$24.95 CAN $17.95 US
☐ El Salvador	$22.95 CAN $14.95 US
☐ Guadeloupe	$24.95 CAN $17.95 US
☐ Guatemala	$24.95 CAN $17.95 US
☐ Hawaii	$29.95 CAN $21.95 US
☐ Honduras	$24.95 CAN $17.95 US
☐ Islands of the Bahamas	$24.95 CAN $17.95 US
☐ Las Vegas	$17.95 CAN $12.95 US
☐ Lisbon	$18.95 CAN $13.95 US
☐ Louisiana	$29.95 CAN $21.95 US

Ulysses Due South

☐ Acapulco	$14.95 CAN $9.95 US
☐ Belize	$16.95 CAN $12.95 US
☐ Cancún & Riviera Maya	$19.95 CAN $14.95 US
☐ Cartagena (Colombia)	$12.95 CAN $9.95 US
☐ Huatulco - Puerto Escondido	$17.95 CAN $12.95 US
☐ Los Cabos and La Paz	$14.95 CAN $10.95 US
☐ Puerto Plata Sosua	$14.95 CAN $9.95 US
☐ Puerto Vallarta	$14.95 CAN $9.95 US
☐ St. Martin and St. Barts	$16.95 CAN $12.95 US

Ulysses Travel Journals

☐ Ulysses Travel Journal (Blue, Red, Green, Yellow, Sextant)	$9.95 CAN $7.95 US
☐ Ulysses Travel Journal 80 Days	$14.95 CAN $9.95 US

Ulysses Green Escapes

☐ Cycling in France	$22.95 CAN $16.95 US
☐ Cycling in Ontario	$22.95 CAN $16.95 US
☐ Hiking in the Northeastern U.S.	$19.95 CAN $13.95 US
☐ Hiking in Québec	$19.95 CAN $13.95 US

Title	Qty	Price	Total
Name:		Subtotal	
		Shipping	$4 CAN
Address:		Subtotal	
		GST in Canada 7%	
		Total	

Tel: Fax:

E-mail:

Payment: ☐ Cheque ☐ Visa ☐ MasterCard

Card number_____ Expiry

date_____

Signature_____

_____

ULYSSES TRAVEL GUIDES

4176 St-Denis,
Montréal, Québec,
H2W 2M5
(514) 843-9447
fax (514) 843-9448

305 Madison Avenue,
Suite 1166,
New York, NY 10165

Toll free: 1-877-542-7247
Info@ulysses.ca
www.ulyssesguides.com